Editor-In-Chief
Uttam Gaulee

Volume 6 No 1 May 2022
JOURNAL OF UNDERREPRESENTED & MINORITY PROGRESS

A Biannual International Refereed Journal

Access this journal online at; http://ojed.org/jump

2022 by *Journal of Underrepresented & Minority Progress*

All rights reserved. This journal or any portion thereof may not be reproduced or used in any manner whatsoever without the express written permission of the publisher/editor except for the use of brief quotations in a book review or scholarly journal. This journal is a STAR Scholars Network publication and Open Journals in Education.

Published by: STAR Scholars Network

Disclaimer

Facts and opinions published in *this journal* express solely the opinions of the respective authors. Authors are responsible for their citing of sources and the accuracy of their references and bibliographies. The editors cannot be held responsible for any lacks or possible violations of third parties' rights.

Journal of Underrepresented & Minority Progress
Volume 6, No 1 (2022)

Advisory Board

Glenda Prime, Morgan State University, USA
Sean Robinson, Morgan State University, USA
Anita Hawkins, Morgan State University, USA
Suresh Ranjan Basak, Metropolitan University, Bangladesh
Drona Rasali, University. of British Columbia, Canada

Editorial Board

Founder/Editor-in-Chief: Uttam Gaulee, Morgan State University, USA
Editor: Muhammad Sharif Uddin, Morgan State University, USA
Managing Editor: Norin Taj, University of Toronto, Canada
Production Editor: Ashmi Desai, San Francisco State University, USA
Publication Editor: Tanjin Ashraf, Australian Catholic University, Australia
Editorial Assistant (Social Media): Samikshya Bidari, Tohoku University, Japan
Editorial Assistant (communication): Sara Domínguez Lloria, University of Vigo, Spain

Copy Editors

Emily Wilkins, University of Dayton, USA
Henry Linck, Morgan State University, USA
Justine Jun, University of Toronto, Canada
Megan Schutte, Community College of Baltimore County, USA
R. Jerome Anderson, Morgan State University, USA

Associate Editors

Antigoni Papadimitriou, Johns Hopkins University, USA
Benjamin Welsh, Morgan State University, USA
Brea Banks, Illinois State University, USA
Dia Sekayi, Morgan State University, USA
Fred Kofi Boateng, University of Ghana, Ghana
Ishrat Ibne Ismail, Shahjalal University of Science & Technology, Bangladesh
Jeevan Khanal, Nepal Open University, Nepal
Masha Krsmanovic, University of Southern Mississippi, USA
Mousumi Mukherjee, O. P. Jindal University, India
Robin Spaid, Morgan State University, USA
Russell Davis, Morgan State University, USA

Ramon B. Goings, Loyola University, USA
Thurman Bridges, Morgan State University, USA

Editorial Review Board

Amanda Wilkerson, University of Central Florida, USA
Andrea Smith, University of West Georgia, USA
Ashley Marshall, North Carolina A & T University, USA
Bhim Bahadur BK, CSI, USA
Carla R. Jackson, Morgan State University, USA
Elizabeth D. Tuckwiller, George Washington University, USA
Felicia A. Shanklin, Southern New Hampshire University (SNHU), USA
Fernando Almeida, University of Porto & INESC TEC, Portugal
Geoffrey Gathii Njenga, Media & Communication Lecturer, Kenya.
Harriet B. Fox, The George Washington University, USA.
Irene Irudayam, Anna Maria College, USA
Jerry Parker, Southeastern Louisiana University, USA
Lynell Hodge, University of Central Florida, USA
Laerke Anbert, University of Copenhagen, Denmark
L. Erika Saito, National University, USA
Mattyna Stephens, Texas State University, USA
Maanasa Gurram, University of Maryland-College Park, USA
Miracle Chukwuka-Eze, Morgan State University, USA
Misty So-Sum Wai-Cook, National University of Singapore, Singapore
Milan Shrestha, Kathmandu University, Nepal
Mukti Thapaliya, University of Canterbury, New Zealand
Mwongela Mikwa, The New School University, USA
Natasha Ramsay-Jordan, University of West Georgia, USA
Norin Taj, University of Toronto, Canada
Pitambar Acharya, Tribhuvan University, Nepal
Prabin Shrestha, Tribhuvan University, Nepal
S. Renee Jones, Middle Tennessee State University, USA
Regina M. Moorer, Alabama State University, USA
Rajendra Joshi, Kathmandu University, Nepal
Rumi Roy, Lakehead University, Canada
Shahinaz Alkhaldi, Morgan State University, USA
Sydney Freeman Jr., University of Idaho, USA
Valerie Riggs, Morgan State University, USA
Vanessa Dodo Seriki, Morgan State University, USA
Wauseca Briscoe, Morgan State University, USA

Journal of Underrepresented & Minority Progress
http://ojed.org/index.php/jump

Aims & Scope

The *Journal of Underrepresented & Minority Progress* (JUMP) features narratives, theoretical and empirically-based research articles, reflections, and book reviews relevant to the progress of minority and underrepresented populations in and across social and national contexts. The Journal encourages the submission of manuscripts by scholars and practitioners in any relevant academic fields, including sociology, psychology, higher education, philosophy, education, and cultural studies. JUMP is indexed in major databases.

An interdisciplinary, peer-reviewed publication dedicated to sharing knowledge about the progress of minority and underrepresented communities in and across different social and national contexts, the *Journal of Underrepresented and Minority Progress* (JUMP) aims to advance knowledge about the progress of marginalized communities through theoretical and empirically-based research articles, book reviews, narrative essays, and reflective writing about positive changes and challenges, emerging policies and practices.

The journal is international in scope and includes work by scholars in a wide range of academic fields including psychology, religion, sociology, business, social work, anthropology, and philosophy. The journal's audiences include scholars and researchers of social sciences focusing their work on issues such as ethnicity and race, caste and class, religion and spirituality, gender sexual orientation, power and privilege, wealth and income, health and wellbeing, beliefs and value systems, and intersections of these issues.

JUMP publishes fully open access journals, which means that all articles are available on the internet to all users immediately upon publication. Non-commercial use and distribution in any medium is permitted, provided the author and the journal are properly credited. All articles published by JUMP are licensed under a Creative Commons Attribution-NonCommercial-NoDerivs 3.0 Unported License.

For questions –

Editor-in-Chief: Uttam Gaulee, Ph.D. E-mail: uttam.gaulee@morgan.edu

OJED
OPEN JOURNALS IN EDUCATION

High-quality, peer-reviewed academic journals based at leading universities worldwide.

Open Journals in Education (OJED) publishes high quality peer reviewed, openaccess journals based at research universities. OJED uses the Open Journal System (OJS) platform, where readers can browse by subject, drill down to journal level to find the aims, scope, and editorial board for each individual title, as well as search back issues. None of the OJED journals charge fees to individual authors thanks to the generous support of our institutional sponsors.

OJED journals are required to be indexed in major academic databases to ensure quality and maximize article discoverability and citation. Journals follow best practices on publication ethics outlined in the COPE Code of Conduct. Journals work to ensure timely decisions after initial submission, as well as prompt publication online if a manuscript is accepted for publication. OJED journals benefit from the editorial, production, and marketing expertise of our team of volunteers. Explore our OJED Journals at www.ojed.org

Journal of Underrepresented & Minority Progress	Higher Education Politics & Economics	JOURNAL OF INTERNATIONAL STUDENTS
THE JOURNAL OF COMPARATIVE & INTERNATIONAL HIGHER EDUCATION	JOURNAL OF INTERDISCIPLINARY STUDIES IN EDUCATION	International Journal of Multidisciplinary Perspectives in Higher Education

TABLE OF CONTENTS

Journal of Underrepresented & Minority Progress
Volume 6, No 1 (2022)
www.ojed.org/jump

EDITORIAL

Egocentrism and Critical Awareness
Muhammad Sharif Uddin, Uttam Gaulee

ARTICLES

Sl	Title and author(s)	Pages
1	Perceptions of Microaggressions and Color-Blind Racial Attitudes among College Students *Brea M. Bank, and Alexandra V. Horton*	1-21
2	Unheard Voices: Transformative Workplace Learning and Support Experiences of Racialized Migrant Women English Instructors in Ontario Higher Education in Canada *Justine Jun*	22-51
3	An Exploration of Black College Students' Conformity to Gender-Role Norms on Gender-Role Stress and Depression *April T. Berry and Lina J. M. Holloway*	52-72
4	Work-Life Management Challenges for Graduate Students of Color at an HBCU During a Pandemic *Sharlene Allen Milton, Nia Caldwell, Deval Popat, Tavril Prout, and Cherese Godwin*	73-96
5	Limbu Poets' Experiences of Using Facebook for Promoting Endangered Indigenous Language *Dig Dhoj Lawati and Karna Rana*	97-120

BOOK REVIEW

Sl	Title and Reviewer	Pages
1	Recent Perspectives on Task-Based Language Learning and Teaching *Krishna Kumari Upadhayaya*	121-124

Editorial

© *Journal of Underrepresented and Minority Progress*
Volume 6, Issue 1 (2022), pp. viii-x
ISSN: 2574-3465 Print/ ISSN: 2574-3481 Online
http://ojed.org/jump

Egocentrism and Critical Awareness

Muhammad Sharif Uddin
Uttam Gaulee
Morgan State University, USA

In a recent interview Ukraine's president Volodymyr Zelensky, stated that the current conflict between his country and Russia is not between two armies or two countries, but rather between two ideologies. One ideology was a free world, free thought, and respect for others. The other ideology, on the other hand, was all about dominating others by using muscle to instill dread and horror in them. His remark was thought-provoking, and it made us reflect on the global culture of superiority complex. Some people believe they are entitled to more advantages than those who are not like them for one or more reasons. Their socioeconomic level, color, gender, culture, religion, and other factors could all be influencing factors.

One of the most important factors in determining superiority or inferiority is socioeconomic position. People in positions of financial and political power expect special treatment in society. Even someone of the same race with a lower socioeconomic standing does not have access to the same advantages and superiority. Furthermore, privileged individuals are still oblivious that they have an unfair advantage in society and can exert power over others. They assume they are acting appropriately. Social instability and chaos result from this narcissistic superiority mindset. Around 150 years ago, Nobel Laureate Bengali poet Rabindranath Tagore wrote "Dui Bigha Jomi," a poem reflecting the face of social authority and control. The poet addressed how society's dominant people took advantage of the weak and destitute. Tagore believed that the affluent appeared to have the right to steal anything from the poor and weak, making them more vulnerable and inadequate.

For years, leaders like President Zelensky and thinkers like poet Tagore have been pointing out inequality on the global arena, in society, and in our daily lives, and calling for change activism. Do we, however, notice the fundamental differences? Do all persons enjoy the same benefits? Are we secure on the streets, in the malls, or at the grocery stores? Are our kids safe in schools? How can we make the world a more humane place? Everyone should be aware of what academics and leaders tell us about humanity on a regular basis. We must understand the core causes of harmful and life-threatening actions on a regular basis around the world. Hate crimes and social dominance are on the rise, as are infectious diseases. Many people are mentally paralyzed for the basic psychological needs of security, food, and shelter. Even the powerful are scared and insistent to gain greater privileges and create social turmoil.

Critical awareness is essential to mitigate the dangerous contagious diseases of hegemonic injustice. Critical awareness is the knowledge, dispositions, and skills that can help an individual analyze, synthesize, and evaluate the common practices in our society and determine what the ideal practices should be. When individuals can recognize the differences between every day and ideal behaviors, they can become the transformative intellectuals that our society sorely needs. This critical knowledge can help disadvantaged groups comprehend their rights and privileges, as many do not recognize they are controlled by others rather believe they are not entitled to the same rights as others because of their social rank, race, or other reasons. In addition, the privileged groups will be able to acknowledge their dominance and accept everyone's equal rights. Their understanding will help them to be respectful to others. As a result, critical awareness will turn every individual into a transformative intellectual, resulting in societal cultural order.

When I (Uddin) was a doctoral student, one of my professors used to say in every class that we need good education as this education is the only medication for all social diseases like domination, injustice, anarchy, and bad politics. He also proposed that our education systems be rebuilt to help young people become advocates for social and global equality, safety, and security. An excellent education, according to that professor, can foster empathy, sympathy, and academic achievement. It is the only way to address everyday issues such as social anarchy, health issues, and political and social imbalances. As a result, successful education is the learning process that fosters people's cognitive growth as well as their social, emotional, and ethical growth. We connect good education to John Dewey's whole-child development process through experiential learning. Experiential learning is a type of learning in which students learn by doing, allowing them to obtain the knowledge, attitudes, and abilities needed to address everyday situations. This knowledge can aid us in comprehending President Zelensky's two ideologies as well as Tagore's societal dominance.

The Journal of Underrepresented and Minority Progress is a free online publication that promotes and publishes practical scholarships that help underrepresented individuals advance academically, socially, and economically. It is an open access, peer-reviewed journal for both writers and readers. Our goal is to empower everyone, both powerful and powerless, to create a better society in which we may all live freely, happily, and safely.

MUHAMMAD SHARIF UDDIN, EdD, is the Journal of Underrepresented & Minority Progress's editor, and a faculty member in the Department of Teacher Education and Professional Development at Morgan State University, USA.

UTTAM GAULEE, PhD, is the Editor-in-Chief of the Journal of Underrepresented & Minority Progress, President of the STAR Scholars Network, and a professor in the Department of Advanced Studies, leadership, and Policy at Morgan State University, USA.

Peer-Reviewed Article

© *Journal of Underrepresented and Minority Progress*
Volume 6, Issue 1 (2022), pp. 1-21
ISSN: 2574-3465 Print/ ISSN: 2574-3481 Online
http://ojed.org/jump

Perceptions of Microaggressions and Color-Blind Racial Attitudes among College Students

Brea M. Banks
Alexandra V. Horton
Illinois State University, USA

ABSTRACT

We examined the relation between color-blind racial attitudes (i.e., the perspective that race should not and does not matter; Neville et al., 2007) and perceptions of microaggressions (i.e., identity-based insults) among students at Predominantly White Institutions, as the literature suggests that experiences with these transgressions may be heightened for Students of Color attending these universities. After completing survey items and being exposed to several vignettes, participants were asked to rate the degree to which they found the scenarios offensive or problematic. Results of the study suggest that individuals who hold stronger color-blind racial attitudes are less likely to perceive microaggressive situations as offensive. Implications for addressing microaggressions particularly among white students in higher education holding color-blind attitudes are addressed.

Keywords: color-blind racial attitudes, microaggressions, higher education

LITERATURE REVIEW

Pierce (1970) first used the term microaggression to describe subtle, unconscious, and automatic putdowns that Black individuals regularly receive from their white counterparts. Today, researchers broadly define microaggressions as verbal, behavioral, or environmental insults that are directed at individuals who hold marginalized identities and are acts of oppression that occur as a result of institutional and systemic inequities (Sue et al., 2007). Although microaggressions are often administered unintentionally, as they are at times meant as compliments, jokes, or conversation starters, these transgressions may have a negative impact on those receiving them (Sue et al., 2007). Microaggressions can take many forms and can come from many different sources. For example, individuals may receive microaggressions from strangers, while these insults may also be disseminated from individuals a receiver regularly interacts with, such as family, friends, classmates, or professors. Microaggressions can be based on any or multiple marginalized identity a person holds (e.g., gender alone, sexual orientation and disability), while the focus of the current paper is on race-based microaggressions and the experiences of People of Color. Researchers have categorized microaggressions as microassaults, which are intentional and conscious behaviors or comments (e.g., using a racial slur), microinsults which are demeaning comments or actions (e.g., saying that someone is a credit to their race due to their achievements), and microinvalidations which negate or ignore an individual's feelings or experiences (e.g., commenting that not everything is about race; (Sue et al., 2007). Racial microassaults are better conceptualized as outright racism and are deemed less socially acceptable. Microinsults and microinvalidations fit better with the definition of microaggression and are the focus of the current study.

Aside from racial microaggressions, color-blind racial attitudes are another focus of the current study. Such attitudes refer to perspective that one should not acknowledge race, but instead should focus on similarities among individuals (Neville et al., 2007). Our culture's shift to preference for color-blind racial attitudes emerged during the transition from the Jim Crow to Post Civil Rights era, in which we saw society push for equality and to eradicate racial bias. Although we acknowledge that this frame of thinking was well-intentioned, a color-blind perspective ignores the lived experiences of those holding racialized identities, as macro- and micro-level racial injustice did not end following the Civil Rights Movement. Research suggests that individuals continue to hold color-blind racial attitudes today (Neville et al., 2007), and for the purpose of the current study, we were interested in examining how these attitudes are related to individuals' perceptions of racial microaggressions, which we know to negatively impact those on the receiving end.

The Impact of Microaggressions

A significant number of research studies have been conducted to examine the negative impact of microaggressions. Sue and colleagues (2007) discuss the dilemma of managing microaggressions, as receivers must make sense of what occurred and decide whether or not to respond. Either choice may lead to a negative outcome for the receiver. When choosing to provide feedback, receivers must then manage defensive or dismissive responses from those who harmed them. On the other hand, a decision to withhold their true feelings may result in loss of self-integrity. Both of these experiences may contribute to "racial battle fatigue," which points to the physiological and psychological stress People of Color deal with when managing race-based microaggressions (Smith et al., 2007). More specifically, racial battle fatigue is associated with anxiety, sleep difficulties, hypervigilance, withdrawal, and anger in People of Color (Smith et al., 2007).

In an experimental study conducted by Wong-Padoongpatt and colleagues (2017), researchers studied the impact of racial microaggressions on Asian American individuals depending on the race of the perpetrator. Researchers found that experiencing microaggressions, particularly from white people as opposed to Asian American individuals, negatively influenced self-esteem and increased stress. Further, Nadal and colleagues (2014) have also found that experiences with microaggressions are related to symptomology of depression, anxiety, and other mental health concerns particularly among People of Color. Later research by the same author suggests that microaggressions do not only impact mental health, but are related to worse physical health, with setting (e.g., school, workplace) playing a role in the type of health concern (Nadal et al., 2017).

Relevant to the purpose of the current study, we know that experiences with microaggressions can also impact university students' perceptions of campus climate. A great deal of research has been conducted to examine the impact of school climate on student success, which Thapa and colleagues (2013) state is "based on patterns of people's experiences of school life and reflects norms, goals, values, interpersonal relationships, teaching and learning practices, and organizational structures" (p. 358). Much of this literature has focused on K-12 schools and has noted several academic and social-emotional benefits of a positive school climate, where students feel safe and respected in the learning environment (Thapa et al., 2013). Although a different setting, these findings can be applied to university campuses. Researchers emphasize the importance of how individuals view the campus, as climate is "a function of what one has personally experienced, but also is influenced by perceptions of how members of the academy are regarded on campus" (Rankin & Reason, 2005, p. 52). Results of research studies suggests that students holding marginalized racial identities experience the campus climate differently than their white counterparts. Specifically, given experiences with racism and harassment, Students of Color at Predominantly White Institutions have identified their campus climates as hostile in comparison to their white peers (Hurtado & Ponjuan, 2005; Rankin & Reason, 2005).

Blatant instances of racism, however, are not the only experiences that negatively impact the way Students of Color perceive their campuses, as research suggests that microaggressions play a role in shaping the way individuals view climate. For example, Solórzano and colleagues (2000) used focus group interview data to examine the microaggressive experiences of African American students on a college campus. Researchers were particularly interested in how these experiences impacted the functioning of students. Participants endorsed experiences of blatant discrimination that contributed to their interpretation of their university as hostile, and also noted that their experiences with racial microaggressions in academic and social spaces made them feel unwelcome on campus. Similarly, as part of a large study at their institution, Harwood and colleagues (2012) conducted focus groups with African American, Asian American, Latino, and Native American students. Participants discussed their experiences with microaggressions, as researchers identified more than 70 racial microaggressions that students reported experiencing regularly on campus. These microaggressions were verbal, behavioral, and environmental in nature and occurred across all spaces on campus, including classrooms, residence halls, and study areas. These experiences with microaggressions were associated with negative perceptions of campus climate, which can impact student retention and engagement (Brezinski et al., 2018).

Potentially most relevant to the college student experience, microaggressions may directly impact students' ability to learn effectively. Some research suggests that individuals experience an immediate depletion in cognitive resources as a result of experiencing microaggressions. For example, although they did not label the manipulation as a microaggression, Murphy and colleagues (2013) found that exposure to subtle racism had a greater impact on the depletion of cognitive resources in Black college students, as compared to instances of blatant racism. Bair and Steele (2010) also found direct links between exposure to prejudiced encounters and diminished cognitive functioning in Black college students, although this was only relevant for participants who reported high levels of racial centrality (i.e., race is an important part of my self-concept). Finally, in a study conducted by (Banks & Cicciarelli, 2019), researchers found that college Students of Color who were exposed to a racially derogatory term experienced diminished cognitive functioning when compared to their white counterparts. Taken together, students on the receiving end of microaggressions are clearly at a disadvantage on the college campus, as they have to manage constant exposure to these insults that may directly impact their physical, psychological, social-emotional, and cognitive functioning. Although research has not explored this relationship, it may be the case that exposure to racial microaggressions directly impacts the degree to which Students of Color persist and reach their academic goals at Predominantly White Institutions, given what we know about campus climate and retention (Rankin & Reason, 2005).

Color-blind Racial Attitudes

As mentioned previously, color-blind racial attitudes encompass the idea that "race should not and does not matter" (Neville et al., 2007). Although the first part of this idea is well-intentioned, the latter part ignores and diminishes the experiences and lived reality of those who hold marginalized racial identities. Race is a noticeable characteristic that triggers immediate preconceived notions, ideas, and previous experiences. To argue that race is not important ignores oppression and injustices that those with marginalized racial identities have historically and are currently experiencing. Although color-blind racial attitudes have received some attention in the literature, few studies using empirical measures of color-blind racial attitudes have been conducted. To fill this gap in the literature, Neville and colleagues (2007) developed and validated the *Color-blind Racial Attitudes Scale* (*CoBRAS*). In their study, researchers found that color-blind racial attitudes were linked to racism and to the idea that white privilege does not exist. Holding the belief that race does not and should not matter does not prevent individuals from holding racial biases that influence how they view individuals with marginalized racial identities. It may also prevent white individuals from recognizing certain advantages they have in life because of their racial background, while simultaneously ignoring disadvantages People of Color may experience.

Color-blind Racial Attitudes and Microaggressions

Some research has explored the connection between color-blind racial attitudes and microaggressions. For example, in a study conducted by Kim and colleagues (2019) researchers explored the relationship between color-blind racial attitudes, as measured by *CoBRAS* (Neville et al., 2007), and the perception of the negative effects of microaggressions in the workplace. Researchers found that white participants with higher ratings on *CoBRAS* (Neville et al., 2007), meaning they held stronger color-blind racial attitudes, were less likely to find microaggressions problematic. Similar to the purpose of the current study, Offermann and colleagues (2014) found that those who held color-blind racial attitudes were less likely to identify microaggressions and blatant racism. This research implies that holding color-blind racial attitudes may influence an individual's ability to perceive or recognize microaggressions. It may also impact an individual's perceptions of microaggressions, making them more likely to find microaggressions less problematic. Finally, Wise (2021) found that for white participants, the negative relation between color-blind racial attitudes and the endorsement of racial microaggressions as offensive or problematic is explained by one's awareness of privilege.

Gaps in the Literature

Although microaggressions have recently received an increasing amount of attention from researchers and have been demonstrated to have negative effects for those on the receiving end, some scholars question the current state of the literature. Specifically, some researchers argue that classifying an act or statement as microaggressive is difficult, as we have not engaged in research to evaluate the degree to which members of a particular group deem a specific action or statement as microaggressive (Lilienfeld, 2017). Further, while one person may label an encounter as microaggressive, another individual holding similar identities may not interpret it the same way and in turn may not experience any negative consequences as a result of exposure (Lilienfeld, 2017). Additionally, a great deal of research on microaggressions has been qualitative in nature, generally through self-report and focus groups. Although some argue that qualitative research should not be the focus, because it lacks a certain experimental rigor (Lilienfeld, 2017; Wong et al., 2014), it is important to note that both qualitative and quantitative forms of research have strengths and weaknesses (Queirós et al., 2017). Further, given several studies demonstrating that negative consequences are associated with microaggressions, it seems the focus should shift towards how to combat these transgressions, rather than determining whether or not some agree about their existence. In addition, examining factors that are associated with microaggressions and individuals' perceptions of them may help determine how to best address them. We were specifically interested in building on previous research (Kim et al., 2019; Offermann et al., 2014) by exploring color-blind racial attitudes as a potential factor that predicts perceptions of these transgressions.

Further, the state of the microaggression literature could benefit from diverse research methodologies. As part of the current study, researchers sought to address this gap by using quantitative methods to examine participant responses to microaggressive exchanges. Lilienfeld (2017) also argues that there is difficulty in determining whether microaggressions are perceived as offensive. Researchers address this issue in the current study by directly asking participants whether or not they found various microaggressive scenarios offensive. Finally, Lilienfeld (2017) and Wong and colleagues (2014) stress the importance of examining individual difference variables that may contribute to one's interpretation of microaggression. This contributes to the issue described earlier surrounding the differential interpretation of these microaggressions as offensive or not. We sought to address this issue by examining the influence of color-blind racial attitudes on participant interpretations of microaggressions as offensive or insulting.

The Current Study

Researchers sought to add to the current literature by examining the relation between color-blind racial attitudes and perceived offensiveness of microaggressions. Although similar research on this topic has been conducted (Kim et al., 2019; Offermann et al., 2014), this study adds to the literature by examining this relation with university students instead of individuals in the workplace. Researchers must engage in scholarship to directly assess how university students interpret microaggressive exchanges, given research suggests these transgressions occur frequently in this setting and may negatively impact students' functioning. Prior to data collection, researchers hypothesized that color-blind racial attitudes would predict the degree to which participants would rate microaggressive encounters as offensiveness. This hypothesis was based on the notion that individuals holding color-blind racial attitudes are less attuned to the offensive nature of the scenarios, and therefore less likely to find them offensive. Researchers were also interested in examining differences in ratings given race and gender. Specifically, we hypothesized that women would rate the microaggressive encounters as more offensiveness than men and that participants of color would rate the microaggressive encounters as more offensiveness than white participants. The hypotheses surrounding race and gender are based on prior research that suggests individuals holding non-racial marginalized identities are better able to detect microaggressions and rate them as offensive (Banks & Landau, 2020).

RESEARCH METHOD

Participants

Participants in the current study included 235 individuals enrolled at a mid-sized, midwestern, Predominately White Institution. Specifically, Students of Color at the institution represented 8% of the student body. Participant age ranged from 18 to 59 ($M = 22.96$, $SD = 6.61$). Participants' self-reported year in school was as follows: 14.5% freshman, 10.6% sophomore, 32.8% junior, 17.4% senior, and 24.7% graduate student. Data regarding race/ethnicity (198 white, 8 Black/African American, 12 Latinx, 9 Asian, and 6 multi-Racial) and gender (55 men, 177 women, 2 non-binary, and 1 other) were also gathered. Two participants did not report their race.

Materials

The *Color-blind Racial Attitudes Scale* (*CoBRAS*; Neville et al., 2007) is a self-report measure of color-blind racial attitudes. The measure includes 20 items that respondents rate on a 6-point Likert scale (i.e., *strongly disagree* to *strongly agree*) that contains three subscales; *Unawareness of Racial Privilege* (e.g., "White people in the U.S. have certain advantages because of the color of their skin") *Institutional Discrimination* (e.g., "Due to racial discrimination, programs such as affirmative action are necessary to help create equality") and *Blatant Racial Issues* (e.g., "Racism is major problem in the U.S."). Research suggests that the *CoBRAS* (Neville et al., 2007) is related to other measures of racial attitudes and that "greater endorsement of color-blind racial attitudes [is] related to greater levels of racial prejudice" (Neville et al., 2007, p. 59). Internal consistency coefficients for the initial examination of the measure were acceptable, ranging from .70 to .86.

Procedure

Following approval from their university's Institutional Review Board, researchers recruited participants through a mass email that was disseminated to all individuals at the university who had opted to receive notifications about research studies. Using the online data collection tool Qualtrics, participants completed a survey that first asked for demographic information, including their year in school, age, gender identity, and race.

Next, participants viewed four scenarios (see Appendix A) that were created by the researchers. Each scenario depicted a woman of color (i.e., African American, Latinx, Asian American, and Native American) receiving a racial microaggression from a white individual with a witness present. Specifically, participants viewed the following four scenarios:

> Scenario 1: Rachel is an African American physics major at Illinois State University. One day while working on a group project with Mark and David, who are both white men, they get on the subject of graduate school. Mark expresses his concern with getting into a program and Rachel sympathizes with him. "Well, you don't have to worry. You'll get in because of affirmative action. You're Black and female, so you hit the jackpot." Mark tells her.
>
> Scenario 2: Lily is a student at Illinois State University who immigrated from China when she was 9 years old. In one of her classes, she has to give a presentation in front of her whole class, something she is not looking forward to, as she hates public speaking. However, the day arrives, and her presentation goes really well. Lily returns to her seat beside her friend Chloe and is feeling great about how she's done. A girl, Holly, who is sitting behind her, leans in and whispers what she intends to be a compliment, "Wow, you did a good job! Your English was really good."
>
> Scenario 3: Taylor is a Latinx student at Illinois State University whose parents are originally from Mexico. One day at lunch with her friends, Nicole and Anna, the three of them began to talk about their Halloween plans. After Taylor shares with them her family's Día De Los Muertos traditions, Nicole, comments, "Wow! That's so cool. I've always wanted to dress up like the Day of the Dead people. Maybe I'll make that my costume this year!"
>
> Scenario 4: Kena is a Native American History major at Illinois State University. She is currently enrolled in a number of history courses including "Colonial Life and Institutions" with her friend Darby. She is particularly excited for this course, as colonial history is her major area of interest. As someone who is deeply rooted in her Native American identity, Kena speaks to the injustices against Native American individuals at the hands of colonial settlers. "I hear you, but I feel like people really need to let that go. Not everything is about

race." Laura, one of her classmates, says after a particularly heated argument.

After reading each scenario, participants indicated whether or not they found the white individual's comments offensive, by indicating "yes" or "no." Participants who responded "yes" viewed a follow-up question that asked them to offer an explanation as to why they found the comment offensive. Additional questions were presented to solicit information surrounding prior exposure to the microaggression described in the scenarios (e.g., Has something like this ever been said to you?). These data (i.e., follow-up and prior exposure items) were not examined as part of the current study. Participants then completed the *CoBRAS* (Neville et al., 2007).

RESULTS

Prior to conducting analyses to address the primary research questions, variables were coded to interpret facilitation. Specifically, a racial status variable was created and coded as 0 for white participants and 1 for participants who reported their racial background as Black, Latinx, Asian, or multiracial. This approach was taken because there were a limited number of participants who indicated a race other than white, given data were collected at a Predominantly White Institution. Gender was recoded as 1 for cisgender women and 0 for cisgender men. Data were not analyzed for those reporting non-binary status or other as their gender, as there were not enough cases to examine differences. Based on the structure of the *CoBRAS* (Neville et al., 2007) outlined in the original study, researchers calculated scores to obtain the *Unawareness of Racial Privilege*, *Institutional Discrimination*, and *Blatant Racial Issues* subscales. The obtained subscales were reliable, as correlation coefficients ranged from 0.83 to 0.94.

Shapiro Wilk tests of normality indicated that the *Unawareness of Racial Privilege* ($W = .96$, $p < .01$), *Institutional Discrimination* ($W = .94$, $p < .01$), and *Blatant Racial Issues* ($W = .88$, $p < .01$) subscale composites were not normally distributed, so nonparametric tests were used to examine these data. Specifically, binary logistic regressions were performed to determine the effects of *CoBRAS* (Neville et al., 2007) ratings on the likelihood that participants found each scenario offensive or not. Results of the analyses indicate that participants providing higher ratings on the *Institutional Discrimination* (e.g., "Due to racial discrimination, programs such as affirmative action are necessary to help create equality") subscale were more likely to rate Scenario 1 and 2 as offensive. Likewise, the *Unawareness of Racial Privilege* (e.g., "White people in the U.S. have certain advantages because of the color of their skin") subscale predicted offensive ratings for Scenario 3, while the *Blatant Racial Issues* (e.g., "Racism is major problem in the U.S.") subscale predicted offensiveness ratings for Scenario 4. Results of these analyses are reported in Table 1. It should also be noted that the Hosmer and Lemeshow analysis across each scenario was not significant, with the exception of Scenario 2. Further, the Nagelkerke R2 values for each scenario demonstrate the *CoBRAS* (Neville et al., 2007) subscales explained at least 26% of the variance in offensiveness ratings (i.e., Scenario 1 = 0.37, Scenario 2 = 0.31, Scenario 3 = 0.26, and Scenario 4 = 0.38).

Table 1:

Binary Logistic Regressions – CoBRAS Predicting Offensiveness Ratings

	B	SE	Wald	p	Exp(B)	95% CI
Scenario 1						
Constant	6.62	0.95	48.33	<.01	748.95	
URP	-0.42	0.29	2.07	.15	0.66	0.38-1.16
ID	-0.98	0.31	9.86	<.01	0.38	0.20-0.69
BRI	-0.07	0.35	0.05	.83	0.93	0.47-1.84
	χ^2	df	p			
H&L	7.53	8	.48			
Model	49.31	3	<.01			
Scenario 2						
Constant	3.98	0.54	54.52	<.01	53.65	
URP	-0.37	0.21	3.17	.08	0.69	0.46-1.04
ID	-0.83	0.23	13.18	<.01	0.44	0.28-0.68
BRI	0.09	0.27	0.11	.74	1.10	0.64-1.87
	χ^2	df	p			
H&L	17.28	8	.03			
Model	57.10	3	<.01			
Scenario 3						
Constant	2.52	0.44	32.75	<.01	12.39	
URP	-0.58	0.19	9.20	<.01	0.56	0.38-0.81

	B	SE	Wald	p	Exp(B)	CI
ID	0.08	0.21	0.13	.72	1.08	0.71-1.64
BRI	-0.54	0.28	3.63	.06	0.58	0.33-1.02

	χ²	df	p
H&L	6.11	8	0.64
Model	49.48	3	<.01

Scenario 4

	B	SE	Wald	p	Exp(B)	CI
Constant	5.48	0.73	55.74	<.01	238.88	
URP	-0.24	0.25	0.96	.33	0.78	0.48-1.28
ID	-0.18	0.28	0.40	.53	0.84	0.48-1.45
BRI	-1.11	0.33	11.15	<.01	0.33	0.17-0.63

	χ²	df	p
H&L	7.32	8	.5
Model	60.51	3	<.01

Note. Unawareness of Racial Privilege = URP, ID = Institutional Discrimination, BRI = Blatant Racial Issues, H&L = Hosmer and Lemeshow

      Before examining the impact of race and gender on participant ratings of offensiveness, analyses were conducted to determine if at least half of the overall sample found each scenario offensive. Results of binomial tests indicated that the proportion of "yes" responses for Scenario 1 (.88), Scenario 2 (.70), and Scenario 4 (.83) was significantly higher than .50, $p < .01$. Significance did not surface for Scenario 3, as the proportion of "yes" responses was .50. Two-way Analyses of Variance were conducted to determine the effect of race and gender on offensiveness ratings. Means and standard deviations are reported in Table 2, and results of analyses are reported in Tables 3 through 6. Significant main effects were identified for gender across scenarios, as cisgender women reported higher offensiveness ratings than cisgender men. Race only significantly predicted offensiveness ratings for Scenario 3, as participants of color reported less offense when compared to their white counterparts. Significant interactions between race and gender did not surface for any of the scenarios.

Table 2:
ANOVA Descriptive Data

	n	M	SD
Scenario 1			
POC cisgender men	10	0.80	0.42
POC cisgender women	25	0.92	0.28
White cisgender men	45	0.73	0.45
White cisgender women	151	0.93	0.26
Scenario 2			
POC cisgender men	10	0.50	0.53
POC cisgender women	25	0.76	0.44
White cisgender men	45	0.49	0.51
White cisgender women	151	0.76	0.43
Scenario 3			
POC cisgender men	10	0.10	0.32
POC cisgender women	25	0.40	0.50
White cisgender men	45	0.36	0.48
White cisgender women	150	0.59	0.49
Scenario 4			
POC cisgender men	10	0.70	0.48
POC cisgender women	25	0.96	0.20
White cisgender men	45	0.78	0.42
White cisgender women	151	0.83	0.37

Note: Scenario 1 = African American woman and affirmative action, Scenario 2 = Chinese woman and English, Scenario 3 = Latinx woman and Día De Los Muertos, Scenario 4 = Native American student and course

Table 3:
ANOVA Comparing Effects of Race and Gender on Offensiveness Ratings for Scenario 1

	SS	df	MS	F	p	η2
Intercept	67.68	1	67.68	684.70	< .01	.75
POC	0.02	1	0.02	0.21	.65	.00
Gender	0.58	1	0.58	5.90	.02	.03
POC*Gender	0.03	1	0.03	0.33	.57	.00
Error	22.44	227	0.10			

Table 4:
ANOVA Comparing Effects of Race and Gender on Offensiveness Ratings for Scenario 2

	SS	df	MS	F	p	η2
Intercept	37.33	1	37.33	185.32	< .01	.45
POC	0.00	1	0.00	0.00	.96	.00
Gender	1.68	1	1.68	8.34	< .01	.04
POC*Gender	0.00	1	0.00	0.01	.95	.00
Error	45.72	227	0.20			

Table 5:
ANOVA Comparing Effects of Race and Gender on Offensiveness Ratings for Scenario 3

	SS	df	MS	F	p	η2
Intercept	12.32	1	12.32	51.94	< .01	.19
POC	1.16	1	1.16	4.88	.03	.02
Gender	1.67	1	1.67	7.04	.01	.03
POC*Gender	0.03	1	0.03	0.12	.73	.00
Error	53.58	226	0.24			

Table 6:

ANOVA Comparing Effects of Race and Gender on Offensiveness Ratings for Scenario 4

	SS	df	MS	F	p	η^2
Intercept	63.42	1	63.42	454.13	< .01	.67
POC	0.01	1	0.01	0.10	.76	.00
Gender	0.59	1	0.59	4.25	.04	.02
POC*Gender	0.25	1	0.25	1.75	.19	.01
Error	31.70	227	0.14			

Finally, researchers examined race and gender as predictors of color-blind racial attitudes using Mann Whitney U tests, given the non-normality of the *CoBRAS* (Neville et al., 2007) data. Results are presented in Table 7. Gender significantly predicted ratings on the *Blatant Racial Issues* and *Institutional Discrimination* subscales, as cisgender men provided higher ratings than cisgender women. Race was a significant predictor on the *Blatant Racial Issues* subscale, as white participants provided higher ratings than participants of color.

Table 7:

Mann-Whitney U Comparing Effects of Race and Gender on CoBRAS Ratings

		n	Mean Rank	Sum of Ranks	Mann-Whitney U	Z	p
URP	POC	35	115.36	4037.50	3407.50	-0.16	.88
	White	198	117.29	23223.50			
	Women	177	112.9	19983.00	4230.00	-1.47	.14
	Men	55	128.09	7045.00			
ID	POC	35	102.41	3584.50	2954.50	-1.35	.18
	White	197	119	23443.50			
	Women	176	105.32	18537.00	2961.00	-4.35	<.01
	Men	55	150.16	8259.00			
BRI	POC	34	96.28	3273.50	2678.50	-1.87	.06

White	197	119.4	23522.50			
Women	175	109.23	19114.50	3714.40	-2.56	<.01
Men	55	135.46	7450.50			

Note. Unawareness of Racial Privilege = URP, ID = Institutional Discrimination, BRI = Blatant Racial Issues

DISCUSSION AND CONCLUSIONS

Research on microaggressions has received increasing attention in recent years, although some researchers argue that the current literature lacks experimental rigor and data that supports researchers' interpretations these transgressions as offensive and insulting (Lilienfeld, 2017; Wong et al., 2014). As part of the current study, researchers sought to address gaps in the literature by (a) using quantitative methods, (b) directly assessing participants' interpretations of microaggressive statements as offensive or insulting, and (c) examining the relationship between color-blind racial attitudes and perceived offensiveness in the microaggressive scenarios. Some evidence supporting research hypotheses surfaced. Particularly, color-blind racial attitudes generally predicted ratings of the scenarios as offensiveness, although this was not the case across all *CoBRAS* (Neville et al., 2007) subscales and scenarios. Nonetheless, results suggest that the more likely an individual holds color-blind racial attitudes, the less likely they are to interpret microaggressions offensive. This finding is consistent with results of previous studies that have identified links between color-blind racial attitudes and diminished sensitivity to microaggressions (Kim et al., 2019; Offermann et al., 2014) and has strong implications surrounding how individuals might respond when they witnesses microaggressions or are identified as perpetrators. Although additional research that specifically addresses the following is necessary, it may be the case that individuals holding color-blind racial attitudes who are less likely to view microaggressions as offensive may be more likely to be dismissive or defensive when responding, further harming individuals holding marginalized identities.

Generally, participants in the study found the scenarios offensive, although this was not the case for Scenario 3. Further, research hypotheses regarding race and gender as predictors of color-blind racial attitudes and offensiveness ratings were partially supported. For all four scenarios, gender differences emerged in participant ratings of offensiveness, as cisgender women found the scenarios more offensive than cisgender men. This finding is consistent with the results of previous research that has demonstrated that women are better able to detect race-based insults when compared to men

(Banks & Landau, 2020). Further, research suggests that women are more empathetic, which may account for gender differences (Rueckert et al., 2011). As another explanation, it may be the case that cisgender women's experiences with gender-based microaggressions may explain why they are better are able to identify microaggressions that are race-based, as they have had their own experiences with microaggressions, albeit directed at a different identity. Going forward, researchers should examine variables that may account for these differences. Future research in this area may also benefit from use of scenarios that are more diverse, as the current study only positioned women on the receiving end of the microaggressions.

A main effect of race only surfaced for the third scenario. This may have been related to the limited sampling of participants of color, as it was difficult to recruit a racially diverse sample, given data collection occurred at a Predominantly White Institution. However, race surfaced as a predictor for the third scenario that examined participant reactions to microaggressive comments surrounding Día De Los Muertos. Interestingly, participants of color provided ratings indicating that they found the scenario less offensive than their white counterparts. Although significant racial differences did not surface for the other scenarios, an examination of the means points to a trend that is consistent with research hypotheses: the mean for offensiveness was higher for participants of color. This difference in results for Scenario 3 suggests that the scenario may have been interpreted differently than the others by participants of color. It may also be the case that white participants provided responses that they deemed socially acceptable (i.e., microaggressions are offensive), which would have increased the means of their ratings across scenarios. As such, in the future researchers should consider the use of social desirability measures to control for this possibility.

Finally, although no main effects for race or gender were identified when examining the *CoBRAS* (Neville et al., 2007) *Unawareness of Racial Privilege* subscale, cisgender men provided higher ratings on the *Institutional Discrimination* and *Blatant Racial Issues* subscales, indicating a greater likelihood to hold color blind racial attitudes as compared to cisgender women. This finding is also consistent with the thought that those who are more likely to experience discrimination that is not race-based, in this case as a result of gender, are better able to detect the occurrence of racism and generally the oppression of People of Color. The finding that white participants endorsed a greater degree of color-blind racial attitudes on these same subscales was not surprising, given People of Color's direct experience with racism and discrimination. However, this may point to the importance of engaging white individuals in discussions about racism and institutional discrimination, given results of the current study indicate that knowledge of these inequities is associated with greater likelihood to endorse microaggressions as offensive.

Limitations and Future Research

Several limitations exist surrounding the findings of the current study. As mentioned earlier, the developed scenarios only presented examples of women on the receiving end of microaggressions. Although this methodology offered consistency and control, it too may have impacted participants' ability to empathize with the receiver, as cisgender women may have found it easier, while cisgender men more difficult. Further, because the current study was conducted at a Predominantly White Institution, researchers were limited in their ability to recruit participants of color to the study. A larger and more diverse sample may have produced better power and distributions that were closer to normal, such that more rigorous analyses to explore the interaction of race and gender could have been explored.

The study was conducted with university students at a Predominantly White Institution, so the findings may be specific to this group and should be generalized to individuals of other age groups or in other settings with caution. The current study adds to the literature in that researchers employed quantitative methods to offer insight into the offensive or insulting nature of microaggressions. Going forward, researchers should consider continued use of quantitative methods to explore microaggressions, but should not dismiss the benefits of qualitative methods that can provide detailed information surrounding the experienced of marginalized groups.

In conclusion, as it continues to be common for universities to take on efforts to address inequities, such as the implementation of trainings and workshops on microaggressions to improve campus climate, institutions must consider research to inform these initiatives. Given the results of the current study, those facilitating workshops and more generally faculty, staff and administrators who are in ongoing contact with students might consider the impact of factors such as color-blind racial attitudes during the development of these workshops or when working with students across other settings. Addressing individuals' knowledge about microaggressions without considering such factors may not produce desired changes in behavior, given these underlying factors may directly contribute to the way individuals interpret microaggressive incidents. In particular, we might consider efforts to produce changes in individuals' color-blind racial attitudes prior to exposing them to content about microaggressions.

REFERENCES

Bair, A. N., & Steele, J. R. (2010). Examining the consequences of exposure to racism for the executive functioning of Black students. *Journal of Experimental Social Psychology*, *46(1)*, 127–132. https://doi.org/10.1016/j.jesp.2009.08.016

Banks, B. M., & Cicciarelli, K. (2019). Microaggressive classroom language and diminished cognitive functioning. *Journal for Multicultural Education*, *13(3)*, 276–287. https://doi.org/10.1108/JME-05-2019-0039

Banks, B. M., & Landau, S. E. (2020). Offensive or Not? Examining the Impact of Racial Microaggressions. *Journal of Underrepresented and Minority Progress*, *15*. https://doi.org/10.32674/jump.v3i2.1808

Brezinski, K. J., Laux, J., Roseman, C., O'Hara, C., & Gore, S. (2018). Undergraduate African–American student's experience of racial microaggressions on a primarily white campus. *Journal for Multicultural Education*, *12(3)*, 267–277. https://doi.org/10.1108/JME-06-2017-0035

Harwood, S. A., Huntt, M. B., Mendenhall, R., & Lewis, J. A. (2012). Racial microaggressions in the residence halls: Experiences of students of color at a predominantly White university. *Journal of Diversity in Higher Education*, *5(3)*, 159–173. https://doi.org/10.1037/a0028956

Hurtado, S., & Ponjuan, L. (2005). Latino Educational Outcomes and the Campus Climate. *Journal of Hispanic Higher Education*, *4(3)*, 235–251. https://doi.org/10.1177/1538192705276548

Kim, J. Y.-J., Block, C. J., & Nguyen, D. (2019). What's visible is my race, what's invisible is my contribution: Understanding the effects of race and color-blind racial attitudes on the perceived impact of microaggressions toward Asians in the workplace. *Journal of Vocational Behavior*, *113*, 75–87. https://doi.org/10.1016/j.jvb.2018.08.011

Lilienfeld, S. O. (2017). Microaggressions: Strong Claims, Inadequate Evidence. *Perspectives on Psychological Science*, *12(1)*, 138–169. https://doi.org/10.1177/1745691616659391

Murphy, M. C., Richeson, J. A., Shelton, J. N., Rheinschmidt, M. L., & Bergsieker, H. B. (2013). Cognitive costs of contemporary prejudice. *Group Processes & Intergroup Relations*, *16(5)*, 560–571. https://doi.org/10.1177/1368430212468170

Nadal, K. L., Griffin, K. E., Wong, Y., Davidoff, K. C., & Davis, L. S. (2017). The injurious relationship between racial microaggressions and physical health: Implications for social work. *Journal of Ethnic & Cultural Diversity in Social Work*, *26*, 6–17. https://doi.org/10.1080/15313204.2016.1263813

Nadal, K. L., Griffin, K. E., Wong, Y., Hamit, S., & Rasmus, M. (2014). The impact of racial microaggressions on mental health: Counseling implications for clients of color. *Journal of Counseling & Development*, *92(1)*, 57–66. https://doi.org/10.1002/j.1556-6676.2014.00130.x

Neville, H. A., Lilly, R. L., & Duran, G. (2007). Construction and initial validation of the Color-Blind Racial Attitudes Scale (CoBRAS). *Journal of Counseling Psychology, 13.* https://doi.org/10.1037/0022-0167.47.1.59

Offermann, L. R., Basford, T. E., Graebner, R., Jaffer, S., De Graaf, S. B., & Kaminsky, S. E. (2014). See no evil: Color blindness and perceptions of subtle racial discrimination in the workplace. *Cultural Diversity and Ethnic Minority Psychology, 20(4),* 499–507. https://doi.org/10.1037/a0037237

Pierce, C. (1970). Offensive mechanisms. In F. B. Barbour (Ed.) The Black seventies, 265-282 Porter Sargent.

Queirós, A., Faria, D., & Almeida, F. (2017). Strengths and limitations of qualitative and quantitative research methods. *European Journal of Education Studies, 3,* 369–387. https://doi.org/10.5281/ZENODO.887089

Rankin, S. R., & Reason, R. D. (2005). Differing Perceptions: How Students of Color and White Students Perceive Campus Climate for Underrepresented Groups. *Journal of College Student Development, 46(1),* 43–61. https://doi.org/10.1353/csd.2005.0008

Rueckert, L., Branch, B., & Doan, T. (2011). Are gender differences in empathy due to differences in emotional reactivity? *Psychology, 02,* 574–578. https://doi.org/10.4236/psych.2011.26088m

Smith, W. A., Allen, W. R., & Danley, L. L. (2007). "Assume the Position . . . You Fit the Description": Psychosocial Experiences and Racial Battle Fatigue Among African American Male College Students. *American Behavioral Scientist, 51(4),* 551–578. https://doi.org/10.1177/0002764207307742

Solórzano, D., Ceja, M., & Yosso, T. (2000). Critical race theory, racial microaggressions, and campus racial climate: The experiences of African American college students. *Journal of Negro Education, 69(1/2),* 60–73. https://www.jstor.org/stable/2696265

Sue, D. W., Capodilupo, C. M., Torino, G. C., Bucceri, J. M., Holder, A. M. B., Nadal, K. L., & Esquilin, M. (2007). Racial microaggressions in everyday life: Implications for clinical practice. *American Psychologist, 62(4),* 271–286. https://doi.org/10.1037/0003-066X.62.4.271

Thapa, A., Cohen, J., Guffey, S., & Higgins-D'Alessandro, A. (2013). A Review of School Climate Research. *Review of Educational Research, 83(3),* 357–385. https://doi.org/10.3102/0034654313483907

Wise, A. (2021). Karen is not a slur: The mediating effect of white privilege awareness on color-blind racial attitudes and microaggression perception (Order No. 28411576). [Master's Thesis, Illinois State University] *ProQuest Dissertations & Theses Global.* Retrieved from https://www.proquest.com/dissertations-theses/karen-is-not-slur-mediating-effect-white/docview/2557838527/se-2?accountid=11578

Wong, G., Derthick, A. O., David, E. J. R., Saw, A., & Okazaki, S. (2014). The what, the why, and the how: A review of racial microaggressions research in psychology. *Race and Social Problems, 6(2),* 181–200. https://doi.org/10.1007/s12552-013-9107-9

Wong-Padoongpatt, G., Zane, N., Okazaki, S., & Saw, A. (2017). Decreases in implicit self-esteem explain the racial impact of microaggressions among Asian Americans. *Journal of Counseling Psychology*, *64(5)*, 574–583. https://doi.org/10.1037/cou0000217

BREA M. BANKS, is an Assistant Professor of Psychology at Illinois State University and is a Licensed Clinical Psychologist in the state of Illinois. She is primarily interested in examining the microaggressive experiences of students in schools. Email: bmbanks@ilstu.edu Twitter: @DocBanks4

ALEXANDRA V. HORTON, is a Ph.D. candidate in School Psychology at Illinois State University who is currently completing her predoctoral internship. Alexandra's work focuses on microaggressions and color- and gender-blind attitudes in STEAM fields and education. Email: avhort1@ilstu.edu Twitter: @AVHorton

Manuscript submitted: ***September 14, 2021***
Manuscript revised: ***January 17, 2022***
Accepted for publication: ***January 18, 2022***

Peer-Reviewed Article

© *Journal of Underrepresented and Minority Progress*
Volume 6, Issue 1 (2022), pp. 22-51
ISSN: 2574-3465 Print/ ISSN: 2574-3481 Online
http://ojed.org/jump

Unheard Voices: Transformative Workplace Learning and Support Experiences of Racialized Migrant Women English Instructors in Ontario Higher Education in Canada

Justine Jun
Ontario Institute for Studies in Education
University of Toronto, Canada

ABSTRACT

Racialized migrant women English instructors in higher education have been an underrepresented minority group of teaching professionals in Ontario, Canada. This study investigates highly experienced racialized migrant women English instructors' workplace learning and support experiences. It aims to reveal how transformative their professional learning experiences are and how transformative their workplaces are in including them as newcomer community members. This article provides the literature review to demonstrate why this study was necessary and preliminary findings answering two research questions to display how equitable and inclusive Ontario higher education workplaces are to these understudied teaching professionals in Ontario. The study findings suggest that online professional communities can create a learning and development space for them by serving their unfulfilled needs in the workplace.

Keywords: Canadian Higher Education, EDI (Equity, Diversity, and Inclusion), English Teacher Education, Migrant Women English Instructors, Ontario Workplace, Transformative Learning

INTRODUCTION

This arts-informed collaborative case study research investigates transformative workplace learning and support experiences of racialized Migrant Women English Instructors (MWEIs) in Ontario higher education in Canada in order to discover their workplace cultures. The literature review in this article holds space for presenting new research territory that this study creates and fills in the teacher education field. The preliminary findings answer two research questions: (1) What are racialized MWEIs' workplace learning experiences? (2) What are racialized MWEIs' workplace support experiences? By answering these questions, this study aims to reveal how transformative and equitable Canadian workplaces are in including racialized MWEIs in post-secondary institutions in Ontario.

The literature review illustrates the following salient points: (1) how the scholarship about migrant English instructors is changing and where this study stands, (2) what the literature reveals about conventional teacher education programs in Ontario that have been the only opportunity for migrant English instructors to access and learn about career outlook, (3) what the current literature argues on migrant professionals' workplace experiences, and particularly (4) what it reports about highly skilled migrant women professionals' workplace experiences. This study fills multiple gaps in the literature: this study (1) reveals how racialized MWEIs who are highly experienced English instructors in Ontario are integrated into its higher education workplaces, (2) describes individual and cultural assets they can contribute to Canadian institutions, differently than in the studies emphasizing their linguistic deficiencies as "non-native English-speaking teachers" (Moussu & Llurda, 2008), and (3) demonstrates that a virtual teacher learning and development community can become an inclusive teacher support space, responding to the studies problematizing conventional teacher education programs with a lack of equitability (Bouhali, 2019; Marom, 2017; Marom & Ilieva, 2016).

This article briefly discusses the theoretical framework for this study, research methods that have been used for data collection, and data analysis methods. The data are currently being analyzed. Hence, this article reports the preliminary findings of Research Questions 1 and 2. Due to the sparseness of the literature on racialized MWEIs' workplace experiences, the study findings will certainly contribute to English teacher education and professional development fields. This study also suggests that a strong online Community of Practice (Wenger, 1998) can serve the target minority group of English instructors in Ontario, Canada, meeting their unmet needs and online collaborative professional communities can be an alternative form of teacher education programs.

LITERATURE REVIEW
Changing Perspectives about Migrant English Instructors
Non-Native English-Speaking Teachers (NNESTs): Deficit-Based Perspectives

Researchers have investigated migrant English teachers addressing them as *Non-Native English Speaking Teachers (NNESTs)* (Braine, 2010; Dogancay-Aktuna, 2008; Kim, 2011; Medgyes, 2000; Moussu, 2006; Moussu & Llurda, 2008). One concept that has divided English language teachers into two categories is *"Native-speakerism"* (Holliday, 2006). Holliday defines *Native-speakerism* as a pervasive ideology in the English language teaching field, believing that *Native English Speaking Teachers (NESTs)* represent a "Western culture" embodying the ideal English language and English language teaching methodology (Holliday, 2006, p. 385). Although scholars like Medgyes (1994) attempted to challenge the binary notion of *NESTs* and *NNESTs,* the term *NNESTs* still imply deficit-based perspectives toward migrant English teachers. As Zhang (2016) mentioned, *NESTs* and *NNESTs* were considered as "two different species" who differed in terms of language proficiency and teaching practices for several decades (p. 322). Researchers' deficit-based perspectives about migrant English teachers result in negative interpretations of their skills and practices. For instance, Tang (1997) argued that *NESTs* were superior to migrant English teachers due to their language skills. Dogancay-Aktuna (2008) reported that English language skills crucially differentiated language teachers' self-perceptions that influence their teaching performance. Faez's (2010) pedagogical suggestions for migrant teachers focused on supplementing the lack of language skills and cultural knowledge rather than supporting them to strengthen their multilingual resources and transcultural assets.

This tendency of binary visions continued to spread until the mid-2000s. Amin (2000, 2005; Amin & Kubota, 2004) identifies these perspectives as "colonialist ideologies of white native speakers as 'owning' English" (Amin, 2005, p. 200). She argues that these deficit-based perspectives intersect with racism and sexism, picturing **"non-white immigrant women" as "permanent Others"** (Amin, 2005, p. 200). Some scholars also argue that these traditional perspectives of othering and negatively labelling different people are "undemocratic" and "unthinking" (Holliday, 2005, p. 19, 2006, p. 386; Kubota, 2001; Pennycook, 2002).

Kerekes (2017) supports this argument stating that the native speaker model is obsolete in today's diverse workplaces, and the "White-Anglo-Christian-Middle-Class prototype" represents the hegemony of the society (p. 417). Jenkins (2000) also endorses the argument by affirming that terms such as *NNESTs* are no longer viable in the language teaching field (pp. 8-9). Other scholars (Canagarajah, 1999; Kubota, 2001; Pennycook, 1994) agreed that using the dichotomized terms would encourage political inequalities. According to Holliday (2006), the undoing of *native-speakerism* is unquestionably necessary for all school communities to eradicate embedded prejudices and ideologies. He argues that all stakeholders can understand "the meanings and realities of students and colleagues from outside the English-speaking West" (Holliday, 2006, p. 386). This study never uses these binary terms reflecting researchers' deep-rooted deficit-based perspectives.

Internationally Educated Teachers (IETs): Asset-Based Perspectives

Rudolph et al. (2015) problematized dichotomic lenses such as *native-speakerism* and the *native speaker fallacy* in research differentiating understanding of *NESTs'* and *NNESTs'* experiences (p. 42). Instead, they applied postmodern and poststructural approaches to address inequality in the English language teaching field and cultivate inclusivity. This *NNEST* movement is a professional movement advocating more participatory, democratic, collaborative, and inclusive practices in the TESOL (Teaching English to the Speakers of Other Languages) field by institutionalizing discourses of multilingualism, multiethnic and multiculturalism (Braine & Selvi, 2018). While scholars in the field request the diversification of voices and empowerment of underrepresented language teachers, they have also recognized systemic obstacles preventing migrant teachers from exerting their resources and assets (Marom, 2019; Pollock, 2015; Pollock, 2010; Ryan et al., 2009). Schmidt and other scholars (Schmidt, 2010; Schmidt et al., 2010; Schmidt & Block, 2010; Schmidt & Gagné, 2015; Schmidt & Janusch, 2016) have investigated and reported inequitable educational policies and programming as systemic barriers resulting in the marginalization of migrant teachers in Manitoba and Ontario. Walsh and Brigham (Brigham, 2011; Walsh, 2008; Walsh & Brigham, 2007; Walsh et al., 2011) have revealed how neoliberalism dominates teaching markets and how migrant women teachers are underserved and marginalized while transitioning from teacher education programs to employments in the Canadian market system. The preliminary findings of this study support these arguments. Racialized MWEIs testify that they have factually experienced inequitable educational policies and practices in their workplaces. Also, neoliberalism-driven competitions are pervasive in some institutions. Colleagues do not share resources and ideas, the toxic working environment causes migrant instructors to burn out, and some of the instructors did not survive in those institutions.

Scholars started arguing that they needed different perspectives to understand "different facets of the complex nature and processes of (language) teacher identity" (Varghese et al., 2005, p. 38). As a result of the shifts in perspectives, the term *NNESTs* has been gradually replaced by *Internationally Educated Teachers (IET)*. Prominent scholars in the English language field generally welcome this new term (Marom, 2019, p. 85). Researchers' approaches to investigating migrant teachers and their professional experiences have been moving away from deficit-based perspectives toward asset-based perspectives. This study is strongly rooted in the latter advocating that employers and teacher educators should acknowledge and value migrant instructors' assets, viewing them as multicompetent language users rather than deficient natives (Cook, 2016, p. 187).

As researchers started exploring migrant language teachers' assets and resources rather than their linguistic and cultural deficiencies, they have applied diverse insights to understanding migrant teachers' professional experiences. Some scholars (Danielewicz, 2001; White & Ding, 2009) noted the importance of the socio-cultural and political context. A group of scholars (Beijaard et al., 2004; De Costa & Norton, 2017; Deters, 2009; Kerekes, 2017; Parkinson, 2008; Sfard & Prusak, 2005; Varghese et al., 2005) highlighted migrant teachers' agency as their strategy to cope with their professional challenges. The preliminary findings of this study also support this argument. Some others (Braine, 2005; Fithriani, 2018; Schmidt, 2010; Selvi, 2018; Soheili-Mehr, 2018; Zhang, 2016) have investigated discrimination issues in migrant instructors' employment and workplace integration. This study also support that these issues still exist. The existing inequalities at work affect both domestic and migrant instructors (Tajeddin & Adeh, 2016, p. 37).

Consequently, this study centers on the researcher's asset-based perspectives toward migrant English instructors aiming to uncover their contributions to Canadian institutions rather than their deficient gaps in linguistic and cultural skills that are perceived to be filled by teacher educators and colleagues from the dominant culture who use English as their dominant language.

Supporting Alternatives for Migrant English Instructors in Ontario

Teacher education programs often become the first educational environment that migrant teachers access and learn about Canadian working culture as immigrant professionals in Canada. They are bridging programs and TESL (Teaching English as a Second Language) programs.

In Ontario, a federal government funded bridging program served migrant English instructors pursuing adult teaching in the province (Citizenship and Immigration Canada, 2008). The researcher was the instructor and the manager of the program between 2013 and 2017. However, the government discontinued the program in 2017 like most other bridging programs in Canada "before the longitudinal impact could be documented" (Schmidt & Janusch, 2016, p. 139). Thus, the literature does not sufficiently support the importance of those bridging programs and their impact on migrant teachers' professional journey. In British Columbia, several scholars have emphasized offering migrant teachers bridging programs in Canada is crucial (Bouhali, 2019; Marom, 2017, 2019; Wimmer et al., 2019). However, no such study has yet been conducted in Ontario. This research is the first study of its kind in the province. All the research participants in the study are the graduates of bridging programs and conventional teacher education programs (TESL programs). They request the government to revive a bridging program for migrant English teachers with no or low cost in Ontario. They attest that their bridging programs critically helped them develop their transcultural understandings of employment and the workplace to pursue their teaching career in Canada and become better prepared for higher education teaching environments.

Scarce literature discusses the influences of bridging programs and TESL programs in Ontario on migrant teachers. However, this literature review manifests that (1) non-existent government support for migrant English instructors results in no support for this minority group of English instructors falling in the crack within the Canadian employment system and (2) the TESL programs which are the only other option for them to access in the province are questioned concerning Equity, Diversity, and Inclusion (EDI) issues. These instructors are presently left alone in the system. This research portrays how difficult it is for them to individually fight against the systemic barriers and inequitable treatments from colleagues and managers. New supporting alternatives for currently working migrant English instructors should be considered because of their different needs. In the findings section, this research suggests an online collaborative professional development community as an alternative form of teacher education program, which is unconventional but necessary for migrant English instructors in Ontario higher education. The following review summarizes the literature on bridging programs and TESL programs in Ontario.

Bridging Programs

In the mid-2000s, the Canadian government started offering numerous bridging programs for internationally educated teachers. Most of the bridging programs were provided in cooperation with universities, school boards, provincial and federal agencies to respond to the increasing number of migrant professionals in the Canadian employment market and simultaneously improve a teacher shortage in Ontario declared by 2007 (Janusch, 2015; Schmidt et al., 2010; Schmidt & Janusch, 2016). However, as the English teaching market was rapidly saturated with an oversupply of English teachers, employment opportunities for migrant teachers quickly decreased. The governments then began discontinuing these bridging programs in the late 2000s.

In Manitoba, Schmidt et al. (2010) reported that the government policies caused systematic inequities and inefficiencies in implementing a bridging program for migrant teachers. The scholars manifested the evidence of systemic barriers such as resistance from the faculty members of well-established teacher education programs, school departments, and the government departments relevant to funding issues (Schmidt et al., 2010, p. 450). These scholars problematized immigrant education agendas based on immediate economic gains, deficit perspectives of hiring authorities, and inequitable and insensible school communities, eventually underserving migrant teachers systemically (Schmidt et al., 2010, p. 450). Schmidt and Janusch (2016) were critical of "neoliberal assimilationist policies" and the tendency to regard employment rates as the most valued indicator of the success of bridging programs (pp. 139, 149). As a result, educational policies centered around economic perspectives and the resistance from well-established teacher education programs became systemic barriers to migrant teachers.

Migrant teachers highly value teaching practicum experiences in bridging programs as the opportunities to learn Canadian ways of teaching, culture, and classroom management (Beynon et al., 2004; Cruickshank, 2004; Myles et al., 2006; Shervey & O'Byrne, 2006; S. Walsh & Brigham, 2007). Janusch's study (2015) reiterates the value of a teaching practicum in a bridging program preparing migrant teachers for their real workplace experiences. Yet, Deters (2015) highlights that only a few migrant teachers could benefit from bridging programs, eventually marginalizing those who could not access these programs as well (p. 428). Deters (2015) also warns that no funding for bridging programs is offered when the market experiences an over-supply of teachers (p. 428). As a result, the Canadian governments' discontinuing bridging programs has magnified the systemic marginalization of migrant teachers.

TESL Programs

TESL Canada and TESL Ontario programs play the most significant role in educating migrant English instructors teaching adults in Ontario. These programs function as re-credentialing pathways to employment for migrant instructors. For this reason, many teacher educators in the TESL field and career advisors in settlement agencies often recommend that migrant English instructors enroll in these certification programs to transition their teaching careers successfully. However, many scholars agree that the teacher certifying process is only the beginning of multiple layers of obstacles and challenges for migrant teachers until they are acknowledged and valued as qualified and legitimate language teachers in Canada (Benyon et al., 2004; Bouhali, 2019; Cho, 2010; Cruickshank, 2004; Deters, 2015; Marom, 2017; Marom & Ilieva, 2016; Mwebi & Brigham, 2009; Niyubahwe et al., 2013; Phillion, 2003; Schmidt, 2010; Soheili-Mehr, 2018; Walsh et al., 2011; Wimmer et al., 2019; Zhao, 2012). Scholars also advocate that teacher education programs need transformation to be more inclusive and equitable for migrant teachers (Benyon et al., 2004; Bouhali, 2019; Cho, 2010; Marom, 2017; Marom & Ilieva, 2016; Phillion, 2003).

Zhao (2012) discovered that migrant teachers experienced genuinely multifaceted challenges and multifold strategies with the implications of racism and discrimination issues in teacher education programs. Sohcili-Mehr (2018) has also verified this finding in his study. Soheili-Mehr (2018) reports that migrant instructors' overseas credentials and their teaching experiences are not valued in the teacher credentialing processes (p. 283). Moreover, most participants reported their experiences of unequal treatment in the certifying institutions or by the hiring authorities (pp. 273-277). His findings describe de-professionalizing (pp. 314-315) and gatekeeping discourses (pp. 314-316) in the TESL programs that impede migrant instructors' professional integration. The research reveals that migrant instructors are forced to conform to the new standards, negotiating their well-established professional identities, while their assets are merely acknowledged or valued (p. 312). However, the instructors often considered learning in the TESL accreditation programs as the only way to gain recognition, acceptance, and legitimacy in their profession in the mainstream professional society. The research participants of this study highly valued the bridging programs they attended rather than the TESL programs because of the practical cultural knowledge and experience they could learn and apply to their current workplaces.

Migrant Professionals' Workplace Experiences

Rare studies discuss migrant English instructors' workplace experiences in higher education. Nevertheless, the current literature informs the findings on the working environment for migrant teachers and professionals: (1) the neoliberalism-driven Canadian employment market and contingent employment arrangements have caused migrant teachers to experience consequential professional challenges and workplace stressors (Deters, 2009, 2011, 2015; Janusch, 2015; Kerekes, 2017; Marom, 2019; Phillion, 2003; Pollock, 2006, 2010; Ryan et al., 2009; Schmidt, 2010; Schmidt & Block, 2010; Schmidt & Gagné, 2015; Schmidt & Janusch, 2016; Walsh, 2008; Walsh & Brigham, 2007; Walsh et al., 2011; Zhao, 2012); (2) discrimination and racism have been major professional stressors that migrant teachers face when integrating into Canadian workplaces (Deters, 2015; Fotovatian, 2012, 2015; Guo, 2013; Pollock, 2010; Schmidt, 2010; Shan & Guo, 2013); (3) mentorship can work as an excellent method of supporting migrant professionals; and (4) what Canadian workplace culture implies but Canadian workplaces do not truly demonstrate in actual practice.

Barriers in the Employment Market

Walsh, Brigham, and Wang (2011) critically analyzed the neoliberalism-driven employment market feeding the existing inequities toward "internationally educated female teachers" in the labour market (pp. 659-661). Their significant arguments include that teacher education is closely tied to "economic production function" (Walsh et al., 2011, p. 659). Researchers identified the following barriers for migrant teachers in the employment market: (1) blocks to gaining Canadian teaching certifications due to competency-oriented criteria (Henley & Young, 2009); (2) obstacles to teaching experiences resulting from administrators' unmitigated control over teachers' work arrangements (Grimmett, 2009); and (3) racial and language-based discrimination in the hiring process and workplace (Walsh et al., 2011, p. 658). Schmidt and her colleagues (Schmidt, 2010; Schmidt et al., 2010; Schmidt & Block, 2010; Schmidt & Gagné, 2015; Schmidt & Janusch, 2016) critique neoliberalism deeply penetrated in the stakeholders' minds such as policymakers implementing educational policies, teacher educators designing courses, and even migrant teacher themselves striving to gain full-time employment as the evidence of their successful integration. Olsen (2015) reiterates Giroux's (2004) argument on how deeply economic perspectives operate in the English teaching community within the framework of "market fundamentalism" (Olsen, 2015, p. 313). While employers hire and support migrant instructors according to their economic capital, those who do not "fit in the system" with "low or unrecognized capital" are marginalized in the employment system (Marom, 2019, p. 92).

Due to non-standard work arrangements (Connelly & Gallagher, 2004, p. 962), migrant teachers experience high degrees of uncertainty (Boyce et al., 2007, p. 6), the improbability of establishing rapport with colleagues, administrators, school staff, and students, and the sense of powerlessness inside and outside of the classroom (Pollock, 2015, pp. 102-103). Pollock's study (2015) explicitly discusses migrant teachers' professional challenges due to their non-standard work arrangements, such as substitute teachers in the workplace. The study findings are highly relevant to the realities of migrant English instructors working with adults. One crucial insight that Pollock (2015) shares is that **the already established continuing professional development model** (Day & Sachs, 2004, p. 3) **is not appropriate** for occasional teachers (Pollock, 2015, p. 104) due to the contingency of their supply and seasonal work arrangements. Instead, Hodkinson (2009) and other scholars conclude that **informal and ongoing professional learning** is a viable option for migrant teachers with diverse needs and work arrangements (Pollock, 2015, p. 104).

The most stressful factor for migrant teachers while transitioning from teacher education programs to Canadian workplaces was employment search (Zhao, 2012, p. 128). Underemployment and unemployment were substantial stressors to migrant teachers, coupled with disadvantageous hiring policies and practices (Zhao, 2012, p. 241). Conflicts and tensions with teacher educators, mentors, and colleagues and the heavy workload were also critical to migrant teachers, contributing to their workplace stressors besides their financial constraints (Zhao, 2012, pp. 241-242). Zhao's findings (2012) display no definite patterns in migrant instructors' professional challenges, stressors, and coping strategies because the complex job market implies different types of obstacles depending on migrant instructors' differing backgrounds, such as career stages, professional experiences, and teaching environments (pp. 238-243, pp. 252-253). Deters (2015) also reports migrant teachers' various professional difficulties and strategies diversified by their individually experienced social, institutional, intercultural, personal, and systemic challenges.

Challenges in Workplace Integration

The researcher's professional experience has demonstrated that migrant instructors with no professional network and personal relationships with local references in Ontario, can easily face professional challenges in their workplace integration. For this reason, part-time and supply teaching, volunteering, teaching in private schools, and attending bridging courses have been the strategies for migrant instructors to develop their professional network (Bascia & Jacka, 2001; Deters, 2009, 2015, p. 427; Pollock, 2010; Ryan et al., 2009; Soheili-Mehr, 2018; Zhao, 2012). Shan and Guo (2013) argue that "immigrants' professional identity is highly contingent on institutional recognition," crucially affecting their employment, promotion, and professional learning (p. 38). The dominant culture and credentials that the "host societies" impose shape migrant professionals' self-perception and workplace learning (Shan & Guo, 2013, p. 38). Deters (2015) emphasized the importance of the receiving community's attitudes (p. 428). Employers, hirers, and administrators can immensely influence migrant teachers' successful professional integration if they embrace diversity and practice inclusivity by actively hiring migrant teachers (Deters, 2015, p. 428). Guo (2013) specifically researched "the glass ceiling" effects (Pendakur & Woodcock, 2010; Wong & Wong, 2006) that "prevent immigrants from moving up to management positions" (p. 112). Besides, **visible minorities experience "racialized disparities"** in their earnings and working conditions due to their ethnic and cultural differences (Guo, 2013, pp. 95, 112). Pendakur and Pendakur (2007) argue that a glass ceiling is genuinely present and **"older and more educated visible minority" participants experience limited access to high-wage jobs,** compared to their "white" counterparts in Canada (p. 58). Fotovatian (2015) asserts that Guo's (2013) 'triple glass effect' is factual in Canadian higher education: "a glass gate blocking entrance to professional jobs, a glass door denying access to high-waged firms, and a glass ceiling to the potential promotion of immigrants to managerial positions" (Fotovatian, 2015, p. 232).

Bascia (1996) examined racialized minority teachers' workplace satisfaction and frustration in Ontario to testify the racism and disparity issues existing in the educational field as policies are put into practice (p. 15). The scholar advocated "changes in administrative and organizational conditions" so that minority teachers and students can be explicitly valued and encouraged to engage in school communities with trust (p. 163). Now, Schmidt (2010) attests that discriminatory structures still exist in Canadian schools, university contexts, the job market, and the salary, prohibiting migrant teachers' inclusion in the system (p. 238). Schmidt's study (2010) is significant because of the following reasons: (1) it problematizes the "neoliberal view" (Giroux, 2004) that migrant teachers' successful workplace integration is solely the individual's responsibility (Schmidt, 2010, p. 235); (2) it challenges school community members' perception of "difference as deficit" (Cummins, 2003); (3) it highlights the existing "systemic discrimination" not actively including migrant teachers in the Canadian education systems (Schmidt, 2010, p. 235); and (4) it urges social and public responsibility with which all the stakeholders should engage in migrant teachers' labour market and workplace issues in Canada. These findings are highly relevant to the preliminary findings of this study. The preliminary findings also manifest that racialized MWEIs in Ontario higher education strongly request **co-responsibility from their colleagues and managers** and their appreciation of the diversity that MWEIs bring to their institutions.

Equity issues are common findings about migrant teachers' workplace integration challenges, such as a lack of ethnocultural equity in educational policies and policy implementation (Schmidt & Block, 2010, p. 18), systematic marginalization of migrant teachers in workplaces by pressing them to accept various temporary work arrangements including unpaid work and inaccessibility to professional development opportunities (Pollock, 2010), and *"NNESTs"* who have always been discriminated and marginalized in English teaching employments (Fithriani, 2018, p. 741). Many migrant instructors strive to overcome their workplace challenges with their persistence and agency. However, their personal agency alone cannot overcome all the constraints resulting from structural and systemic barriers (Deters, 2015, p. 428).

Workplace Learning & Mentorship

Scholars in organizational learning studies identify three factors facilitating workplace learning (Barrette et al., 2007): (1) whether the organization has an organizational learning culture; (2) whether individual employees have the control and decisional latitude over their work; and (3) whether **supportive supervisor communication** is in place. Deters' research in the education field (2006) also displays that when migrant English teachers work with supportive and welcoming supervisors and colleagues, they tend to successfully learn professional language and culture in Ontario while being valued for their diverse and different cultures (pp. 9-16). The preliminary findings of this study re-affirm this finding. Working with open-minded colleagues and supportive managers facilitated more transformative learning experiences for racialized MWEIs, fostered positive workplace experiences for development, and cultivated their sense of belonging.

Scholars in organizational culture studies argue that one way of enhancing organizational culture is to incorporate migrant professionals' intellectual resources into the overall organizational *Intellectual Capital* (Nazari et al., 2011, p. 241). In a similar vein, Canadian organizations have been asked to **engage currently underrepresented women and visible minorities more effectively** in the organizational decision-making processes to eliminate glass ceilings for them (Jain et al., 2012, p. 15). Scholars in organizational learning culture have argued that **interactional leadership** is necessary in higher education if post-secondary institutions aim to promote an organizational learning culture, learner autonomy, and a structural change (Knight & Trowler, 2010, pp. 80-82). Smith and Ingersoll (2004) also suggest **collaborative and interactive teacher support activities** such as workshops, collaborations, support systems, seminars, and mentoring. Besides, Oloo's (2012) study on migrant teachers in Saskatchewan recommends **on-going learning opportunities** for migrant teachers in the workplace to meet their unique needs. Each school may have its own organizational culture and unique demands (Doerger, 2003). Likewise, individual teachers may have unique needs (Oloo, 2012). Both parties' unique needs should conjunctively coincide in a constructive form of instructor learning and support (Oloo, 2012, p. 231). Consequently, the literature supports that ongoing mentorship and interactional professional development programs in the workplace can create substantial learning opportunities for migrant professionals. This argument also applies to racialized MWEIs who are underserved in the system.

Canadian Workplace Culture

It is hard to define Canadian workplace culture and what migrant English instructors learn about it. There is not sufficient literature on this topic. In a broader sense, Canadian culture implies multiculturalism (Courchene, 1996). However, many scholars still question the perceived Canadian values of diversity and multiculturalism recognizing the gaps between educational policies and school practices (Schmidt, 2010; Schmidt et al., 2010; Schmidt & Block, 2010; Schmidt & Gagné, 2015; Schmidt & Janusch, 2016). Some migrant teachers consider a linguistically and culturally diverse community that accepts differences as an aspect of Canadian workplace culture but literature also states that not all school communities welcome migrant teachers as colleagues (Deters, 2006, pp. 10-12). Moreover, Ramjattan (2019) reports that Canadian-born English instructors who are racialized also experience white native-speakerism and inequality regimes toward them in Canadian English language institutions in Toronto. Therefore, community members' collaborative efforts are required to implement a more inclusive and dialectic workplace culture (Deters, 2006). The current movement of *Equity, Diversity, and Inclusion* reflects this long-standing argument.

In business and organization fields, scholars have asserted that inequality and discriminatory practices against professionally qualified immigrants still exist in Canadian workplaces and the hidden discourses of "integration" and "insider-insider device" marginalize migrant professionals from gaining workplace opportunities (Hilde & Mills, 2015, p. 181). Also, the professional labour markets in Ontario, Canada, are culturally regulated to the disadvantage of migrant professionals and Canadian regulating bodies operate licensing processes inequitably resulting in institutionalized cultural marginalization (Girard & Bauder, 2007, p. 35). Thus, Canadian institutional culture marginalizes migrant professionals by limiting their access to appropriate professions compared to Canadian-born and Canadian-trained professionals (Girard & Bauder, 2007, pp. 43-44). Regarding this argument, Soheili-Mehr (2018) in the English teacher education field, has also critiqued that the institutions in Ontario do not recognize or value migrant English instructors' foreign credentials (pp. 17, 48, 259).

Racialized Migrant Women English Instructors

Nova Scotia-based two feminist scholars, Walsh and Brigham (Brigham, 2011; Mwebi & Brigham, 2009; Walsh, 2008, 2017; Walsh & Brigham, 2007; Walsh et al., 2011), have studied visible minority migrant women teaching professionals and their significant professional challenges. The scholars argue that migrant women teachers' position in the teaching market is apparently gendered and highly racialized in the way that their differences are heightened, such as ethnicity and languages (Walsh et al., 2011, p. 663). As Soheili-Mehr (2018) highlighted the discourses of "de-professionalization" in the TESL programs in Ontario (p. 283), these scholars draw attention to migrant women teachers' experiences of "deskilling" in the certifying process, "neoliberal discourses," and the subsequent marginalization that the teacher education programs were reproducing in Maritime provinces (Walsh et al., 2011, p. 663). An anti-racist feminist activist and researcher, Amin (1999, 2000, 2001, 2005, 2011; Amin & Kubota, 2004), also argues that "colonialist ideologies of white English native speakers" consequently discriminate visible minority women teachers from the third world living in the first world as the "speakers of non-standard English" in this English teaching field (Amin, 2005, p. 200). Amin asserts that the binary divisions are the actual reality in this field in Canada and the native-speaker concept is a gendered phenomenon. Amin has disseminated counter-hegemonic and anti-imperialist knowledges relevant to the challenges of minority migrant women English teachers (Amin, 2005, p. 201).

Highly skilled migrant women professionals' career experiences have remained hidden in the international management literature (Al Ariss & Crowley-Henry, 2013) and they have been an under-researched group of professionals in the global mobility study field as well (Colakoglu et al., 2018, p. 276) although they are becoming a rapidly growing global workforce. Gender has been a more significant barrier than their immigrant status limiting their professional advancement beyond the mid-management level (Colakoglu et al., 2018, p. 275). Specific gender-related challenges include discrimination during the job search (Al Ariss, 2010), the probability of accepting underemployment (Liversage, 2009; Meares, 2010), and a double earning penalty (Lopez, 2012; Purkayastha, 2005). Simultaneously, migrant women professionals' domestic responsibilities also obstructed their social network and employment opportunities (Colakoglu et al., 2018, p. 275). Several studies report that HR departments' support appears critical for women professionals to access the workforce (Cerdin et al., 2014; Colakoglu et al., 2018, p. 261). This result is in line with the importance of mentors, experienced colleagues, and administrators who are open to integrating newcomer skilled professionals (Barrette et al., 2007; Beynon et al., 2004; Cruickshank, 2004; Deters, 2006, pp. 9-12; Knight & Trowler, 2010, p. 80; Myles et al., 2006; Shervey & O'Byrne, 2006; Smith & Ingersoll, 2004; Walsh & Brigham, 2007). Although these findings are from the studies in other fields, the preliminary findings of this study also manifest that racialized MWEIs' family responsibilities restricted their employment arrangements and social engagements, and the relationships with HR managers crucially affected their work assignments and successful performance.

THEORETICAL FRAMEWORK

Teacher learning inevitably entails Transformative Learning (Mezirow, 1978). Transformative learning occurs when adults as new community members: (1) learn that their perspectives conflict with existing community members' perspectives; (2) start critically reflecting on emerging perspectives in the specific contextual environment; and (3) critically assess these new perspectives through the social interactions and discourses among the community members. Consequently, the new community members experience "perspective transformation" (Mezirow, 1978, pp. 100-110). Mezirow's Transformative Learning Theory (Mezirow, 2000, 2003, 2009) has informed this study to examine how transformative racialized MWEIs' workplace learning experiences have been and their workplaces are. The theory has also impacted the research methods. Research participants critically reflected on the given research questions and co-constructed their critical discourses about those reflections in the collaboratively constructed Professional Development (PD) workshops virtually offered every month for four months.

DATA COLLECTION & ANALYSIS

Five racialized MWEIs have participated in the study to collaboratively develop a case study. They were recruited among the graduates from Ontario teacher education programs who could corroborate their transformative learning experiences shaping them over time. They interactively facilitated four monthly online PD workshops in collaboration. Each workshop addressed one research question. All participants created artworks after critically reflecting on each research question and its sub-questions. Artworks were used to access unverbalized meanings (Brigham, 2011). Each workshop consisted of two parts: (1) participants' artwork presentations and (2) collaborative interpretations of the presentations and artworks. For the final workshop, participants completed two self-assessment tools examining intercultural interaction competencies and an online survey that the researcher created and customized for this research. Participants then interpreted their own results and, as a group, interpreted other participants' results. The discourses crucially displayed research participants' personal and professional transformations. Thus, the data sources include workshop recordings, researcher's journals, field notes, artworks, self-assessment results, an online survey result, and all the follow-up electronic correspondence. Additionally, initial interviews and a questionnaire provided a detailed profile of each participant. Lastly, participants interviewed the researcher, manifesting the transformations that the researcher had experienced as one of racialized MWEIs and as a researcher. Currently, all the data are being analyzed using inductive and deductive thematic analysis (Nowell et al., 2017). The next section discusses the preliminary findings of the PD workshops 2 and 3, answering research questions 1 and 2.

PRELIMINARY FINDINGS

Research Question 1

Research Question 1 inquires about the workplace learning experiences of racialized MWEIs in Ontario higher education: ***What are racialized MWEIs' workplace learning experiences in Ontario higher education?*** Research participants reflected on two sub-questions and described the learning experiences they had experienced while interacting with their colleagues and managers. The following is the summary of the preliminary findings answering Research Question 1, Sub-question 1: ***What have they learned about their workplace culture?***

1. Canadian workplace culture is not fixed or definitive, but dynamic and continuously changing. And I am part of the Canadian workplace culture.
2. Each institution has its own institutional workplace culture.
3. Diversity:
   a. I am different from them (Canadian-born, domestically educated, unracialized instructors).
   b. I accept I am different. I choose my work to shine and get along with my colleagues.
   c. My voices are unheard. I am different and insignificant.
   d. My difference is not accepted in the Canadian workplace.
4. My home language use at work is not accepted. It is viewed negatively.
5. Collaboration:
   a. Collaboration is not part of the workplace culture in some Canadian institutions. Competition is pervasive in those institutions.
   b. I have developed diverse languaging strategies to survive in this competitive working environment and to gain the information I need to perform my work.
6. Speaking up is part of the Canadian workplace culture which I am not used to practicing.
7. English instructors in higher education are expected to:
   a. be resourceful
   b. have excellent communication skills (e.g., Applying active listening skills, finding the best ways to communicate with each colleague and each manager, making transparent communications, filling the cultural knowledge gap, overtly asking for support and help)
   c. be flexible

8. Informal communication styles are common with which I still experience challenges at times, not because of my language but due to other reasons.

The following is the summary of the preliminary findings answering Research Question 1, Sub-question 2: *How do they describe their workplace learning experiences?*

1. From frustration to acceptance: I was frustrated about being different at first but have gradually accepted the fact that I am different. Thus, I am at a better place now.
2. I apply positive approaches to learning from all the experiences in the workplace, positive or negative.
3. Differences always exist. I focus on the common goals at work.
4. Self-care: I have experienced burnout. Then, I made conscious decisions to take better care of myself and my family. It helped me perform better in the workplace.
5. The diversity of the faculty group matters: I feel more comfortable working in a linguistically and culturally diverse workplace than in a workplace with the colleagues and managers from the dominant culture speaking the dominant language alone.
6. Positive experiences are gained when safe and supportive interactions are facilitated at work.
7. Negative experiences are gained when no support from colleagues and managers are offered and no communication among colleagues are shared despite a heavy workload.
8. I have developed strategies to survive in my workplace over time:
    a. Excellent work performance is the best way to survive in the Canadian workplace.
    b. Languaging strategies are useful.
    c. Honesty and sincerity always work.
    d. Focusing on the common goals helps.
    e. Respecting colleagues' needs and differences – I respect my colleagues' different needs and differences. In the same way, I would like my colleagues to respect my needs and differences.
9. Learning while working: Working is the best PD.

10. I have become a precedent for the second racialized MWEI who is also a visible minority individual – It has been two years since I started working in the current workplace. Another visible Muslim colleague joined. Now, my colleagues do not stare at her as they did at me continuously for the first three months. She is highly welcomed at wok now. I am very happy about that.

These learning experiences that all the research participants shared were transformative, impacting their understanding of their workplace cultures. Their learning experiences were often associated with their feelings and emotions. The findings that stood out among the preliminary findings were (1) racialized MWEIs' agentive strategies to transform negative experiences into positive learning opportunities and (2) their strong commitment to learning while working. In other words, as they teach more than five years in Ontario, they have actively and proactively engaged in multiple forms of learning, including: (1) learning new working cultures and information from diverse sources such as human and material resources; (2) unlearning unilateral ways of teaching; and (3) re-learning professionally useful skills to apply to working with colleagues from diverse backgrounds in the online and hybrid teaching environment. They have emphasized that working is the best professional development opportunity because they learn most efficiently and effectively when the learning is relevant to their present needs. Besides, they were able to gain a sense of belonging when their needs are met through the workplace support from their colleagues and managers but when not, they feel disconnected from their institutions.

Research Question 2

Research Question 2 inquires about the workplace support experiences of racialized MWEIs in Ontario higher education: *What are racialized MWEIs' workplace support experiences in Ontario higher education?* Research participants reflected on three sub-questions and shared their workplace support experiences in the current institutions, particularly about the support from their colleagues and managers. The following is the summary of the preliminary findings answering Research Question 2, Sub-question 1: *Which supports have been valuable to them?*
1. Needs-based leadership: Leadership caring about and serving racialized MWEIs' needs
2. Supportive managers who are approachable, empathetic, patient, positive, and ready to listen and support
3. Equity, Diversity, and Inclusion initiatives

4. Open-minded colleagues who willingly share new resources and information
   5. Institutional support: technology and student support
   6. Stable employment
   7. Online teaching environment with diverse PD opportunities

The preliminary findings of Research Question 2, Sub-question 2, display the workplace supports that have not been much helpful to racialized MWEIs for their professional learning and development: ***Which supports have not been very helpful to them?***
   1. Inequitable policies and practices (e.g., PD opportunities and research funding unavailable to contracted faculty members)
   2. No institutional support
   3. Unhelpful working conditions (e.g., The precarious nature of work for partial-load faculty members)
   4. Managers with unhelpful communication styles
   5. Unsupportive managers who do not acknowledge and/or value instructors' individual values and teaching abilities
   6. Costly PD opportunities in the TESL communities
   7. Discouraging colleagues in the matter of promotion or assignment opportunities

Racialized MWEIs in this study have expressed the changes in the workplace supports that they request, reflecting on their workplace support experiences. The following is the preliminary findings of Research Question 2, Sub-question 3: ***What changes in the workplace support would they like to see?***
   1. Leadership led by the managers with educational background rather than business background who understand instructors' work and recognize their contributions and dedication
   2. Institutional support (e.g., Fixed working hours, Community-building activities)
   3. Needs-based workplace support: When I receive help and support when I need them at work, I gain a sense of belonging. When not, I feel disconnected and alone.
   4. Ongoing EDI (Equity, Diversity, and Inclusion) initiatives: My colleagues' attitudes are changing, especially those from the dominant culture.
   5. A safe and supportive professional community: It is what this research has offered me.
   6. Colleagues' and managers' co-responsibility to include migrant instructors: I have felt alone thinking that it is my

own responsibility striving to adjust to this new working cultural environment. However, I have realized during this research that my colleagues and managers should also share the responsibility with newcomer instructors facilitating more equitable workplace culture.

The research participants have stressed how crucial and valuable needs-based support is for their professional growth. This finding suggests that workplace support should be considered as another form of teacher education because those transformative learning moments have been the most helpful teaching moments to the migrant English instructors, which they have not experienced in conventional teacher education programs in Ontario. Equity, Diversity, and Inclusion (EDI) initiatives have impacted changing the attitudes of their colleagues from the dominant language and culture. Hence, they request on-going EDI practices in the workplace. Supportive and open-minded managers and colleagues have made a big difference in their contributions to their institutions and their sense of belonging. Inequitable policies and practices were highlighted as systemic barriers. While they request colleagues' and managers' co-responsibility to include migrant English instructors in their institutions, they also report that they need a safe and supportive community at work. This study suggests that online professional communities can provide the currently missing space that migrant English instructors need for their professional growth.

CONCLUSION & IMPLICATIONS

This study investigates the assets of migrant English instructors as resources, firmly grounded upon asset-based perspectives toward them. Since the federal government closed a bridging program for this minority group of instructors in the province and conventional teacher education programs have not served them as much as they needed in order to be prepared for the current higher education workplaces, migrant English instructors must find other sources to get help and support they need as they work. This study reports that a more customized and needs-based workplace support can work as an alternative form of teacher education that migrant English instructors seek. Responding to the research participants' unheard voices, this study also reports that the online professional community that the research participants collaboratively developed has widely opened the door for them to use it as a space for their learning and professional growth, particularly in this post-pandemic teaching and learning environment. Many more virtual communities like this strong Community of Practice (Wenger, 1998) can be possible in Canada and in other countries. Their voices inform that Ontario post-secondary institutions have the power to transform their workplace cultures to an environment where managers and colleagues welcome and value the differences and diversity that migrant instructors bring, give equal learning and development opportunities to all instructors whether they are contracted or tenured, and take co-responsibility to include them as their community members. EDI initiatives are necessary to transform the Ontario higher education working environment more equitable and inclusive. With their agentic approaches, racialized MWEIs have made positive transformations in their personal and professional lives, and they continue contributing to their institutions. Their contributions are worth acknowledging and honoring in the current Ontario higher education workplaces in Canada.

REFERENCES

Al Ariss, A. (2010). Modes of engagement: Migration, self-initiated expatriation, and career development. *Career Development International, 15*(4), 338–358. https://doi.org/10.1108/13620431011066231

Al Ariss, A., & Crowley-Henry, M. (2013). Self-initiated expatriation and migration in the management literature: Present theorizations and future research directions. *Career Development International, 18*(1), 78–96.

Amin, N. (1999). Minority women teachers of ESL: Negotiating white English. In G. Braine (Ed.), *Non-native educators in English language teaching* (pp. 93–104). Routledge.

Amin, N. (2000). *Negotiating nativism: Minority immigrant women ESL teachers and the native speaker construct.* [Doctoral dissertation, University of Toronto].

Amin, N. (2001). Nativism, the native speaker construct, and minority immigrant women teachers of English as a second language. *CATESOL Journal, 13*(1), 89–107.

Amin, N. (2005). Chapter Nine: Voices of Minority Immigrant Women: Language, Race, and Anti-racist Feminist Methodologies. *Counterpoints, 252,* 183–204.

Amin, N. (2011). Imperialism and the Domestic Front: In Light of To the Lighthouse. *Philosophy and Progress, 49*(50), 41–64.

Amin, N., & Kubota, R. (2004). Chapter 6. Native speaker discourses: Power and resistance in postcolonial teaching of English to speakers of other languages. In P. Ninnes & S. Mehta (Eds.), *Re-Imagining comparative education: Postfoundational ideas and applications for critical times* (pp. 107–127). Routledge/Falmer.

Barrette, J., Lemyre, L., Cornei, W., & Beauregard, N. (2007). Organizational learning among senior public-service executives: An empirical investigation of culture, decisional latitude and supportive communication. *Canadian Public Administration, 50*(3), 333–354.

Bascia, N. (1996). Inside and outside: Minority immigrant teachers in Canadian schools. *International Journal of Qualitative Studies in Education*, *9*(2), 151–165. https://doi.org/10.1080/0951839960090204

Bascia, N., & Jacka, N. (2001). Falling in and filling in: ESL teaching careers in changing times. *Journal of Educational Change*, *2*(4), 325–346.

Beijaard, D., Meijer, P. C., & Verloop, N. (2004). Reconsidering research on teachers' professional identity. *Teaching and Teacher Education*, *20*, 107–128.

Benyon, J., Ilieva, R., & Dichupa, M. (2004). Re-credentialing experiences of immigrant teachers: Negotiating institutional structures, professional identities and pedagogy. *Teachers and Teaching: Theory and Practice*, *10*(4), 429–444.

Beynon, J., Ilieva, R., & Dichupa, M. (2004). Re-credentialling experiences of immigrant teachers: Negotiating institutional structures, professional identities and pedagogy. *Teachers and Teaching: Theory and Practice*, *10*(4), 429–444. https://doi.org/10.1080/1354060042000224160

Bouhali, C. E. (2019). *Is there a glass ceiling for internationally educated teachers in Alberta? A critical interpretive analysis* [University of Alberta]. https://doi.org/10.7939/r3-kdt6-sb14

Boyce, A. S., Ryan, A. M., Imus, A. L., & Morgeson, F. P. (2007). Temporary worker, permanent loser?" A model of the stigmatization of temporary workers. *Journal of Management*, *33*(1), 5–29. https://doi.org/10.1177/0149206306296575

Braine, G. (2005). *Teaching English to the World: History, Curriculum, and Practice*. Laurence Erlbaum Associates.

Braine, G. (2010). *Nonnative Speaker English Teachers; Research, Pedagogy, and Professional Growth*. Rutledge.

Braine, G., & Selvi, A. F. (2018). NNEST Movement. *The TESOL Encyclopedia of English Language Teaching*, *1*(6). https://doi.org/10.1002/9781118784235

Brigham, S. (2011). Internationally educated female teachers' transformative lifelong learning experiences: Rethinking the immigrant experience through an arts-informed group process. *Journal of Adult and Continuing Education*, *17*(2), 36–50. https://doi.org/10.7227/JACE.17.2.5

Canagarajah, S. (1999). *Resisting Linguistic Imperialism*. Oxford University Press.

Cerdin, J. L., Dine, M. A., & Brewster, C. (2014). Qualified immigrants' success: Exploring the motivation to migrate and to integrate. *Journal of International Business Studies*, *45*(2), 151–168.

Cho, C. (2010). "Qualifying" as Teacher: Immigrant Teacher Candidates' Counter-Stories. *Canadian Journal of Educational Administration and Policy*, *100*.

Citizenship and Immigration Canada. (2008). *Guide to the Enhanced Language Training (ELT for Internationally Educated ESL Instructors) Initiative for Service Provider Organizations*. Citizenship and Immigration Canada.

Colakoglu, S., Yunlu, D. G., & Arman, G. (2018). High-skilled female immigrants: Career strategies and experiences. *Journal of Global Mobility*, *6*(3), 258–284.

Connelly, C. E., & Gallagher, D. G. (2004). Emerging trends in contingent work research. *Journal of Management*, *30*(6), 959–983. https://doi.org/10.1016/j.jm.2004.06.008

Cook, V. (2016). Where Is the Native Speaker Now? *TESOL Quarterly*, *50*(1), 186–189.

Courchene, R. (1996). Teaching Canadian culture: Teacher preparation. *TESL Canada Journal*, *13*(2), 1–16. https://doi.org/10.18806/tesl.v13i2.666

Cruickshank, K. (2004). Towards diversity in teacher education: Teacher preparation of immigrant teachers. *European Journal of Teacher Education*, *27*(2), 125–138. https://doi.org/10.1080/0261976042000223006

Cummins, J. (2003). *Challenging the construction of difference as deficit: Where are identity, intellect, imagination, and power in the new regime of truth? In P. P. Trifonas (Ed.), Pedagogies of difference: Rethinking education for social change* (P. P. Trifonas, Ed.; pp. 41–60). Routledge/Falmer.

Danielewicz, J. (2001). *Teaching Selves: Identity, Pedagogy, and Teacher Education*. State University of New York Press.

Day, C., & Sachs, J. (2004). Professionalism, performativity, and empowerment: Discourse in the politics, policies, and purposes of continuing professional development. In C. Day & H. Sachs (Eds.), *International handbook on the continuing professional development of teachers*. Open University Press.

De Costa, P. I., & Norton, B. (2017). Introduction: Identity, Transdisciplinarity, and the Good Language Teacher. *The Modern Language Journal*, *101*(S1), 3–14. https://doi.org/10.1111/modl.12368

Deters, P. (2006). Immigrant Teachers in Canada: Learning the Language and Culture of a New Professional Community. *AELFE Paper Conference*, 1–16.

Deters, P. (2009). *Identity, agency, and the acquisition of professional language and culture: The case of internationally educated teachers and college professors in Ontario*. University of Toronto.

Deters, P. (2011). *Identity, agency and the acquisition of professional language and culture*. Continuum.

Deters, P. (2015). Factors facilitating the successful entry of internationally educated teachers into the Ontario education system. *Bildung Und Erziehung*, *18*(1), 417–430.

Doerger, D. W. (2003). The importance of beginning teacher induction in your school. *International Electronic Journal for Leadership in Learning*, *7*. https://journals.library.ualberta.ca/iejll/index.php/iejll/article/view/423/85

Dogancay-Aktuna, S. (2008). Non-native English speaking teacher educators: A profile from Turkey. In S. Dogancay-Aktuna & J. Hardman (Eds.), *Global English teaching and teacher education: Praxis and possibility* (pp. 61–82). TESOL Publications.

Faez, F. (2010). Linguistic and Cultural Adaptation of Internationally Educated Teacher Candidates. *Canadian Journal of Educational Administration and Policy*. https://journalhosting.ucalgary.ca/index.php/cjeap/article/view/42783

Fithriani, R. (2018). Discrimination behind NEST and NNEST Dichotomy in ELT Profesionalism. *KnE Social Sciences*, 741–755. https://doi.org/10.18502/kss.v3i4.1982

Fotovatian, S. (2012). Three constructs of institutional identity among international doctoral students in Australia. *Teaching in Higher Education*, *17*(5), 577–588. https://doi.org/10.1080/13562517.2012.658557

Fotovatian, S. (2015). Language, institutional identity and integration: Lived experiences of ESL teachers in Australia. *Globalisation, Societies and Education*, *13*(2), 230–245. https://doi.org/10.1080/14767724.2014.934072

Girard, E. R., & Bauder, H. (2007). Assimilation and exclusion of foreign trained engineers in Canada: Inside a professional regulatory organization. *Antipode*, *39*(1), 35–53.

Giroux, H. A. (2004). Betraying the intellectual tradition: Public intellectuals and the crisis of youth. In A. Phipps & M. Guilherme (Eds.), Critical pedagogy: Political approaches to language and intercultural communication. *Multilingual Matters*, 7–21.

Grimmett, P. (2009). Changing a profession back to an occupation: Implications of the agreement on internal trade (AIT) policy framework on teaching and teacher education. *Inspiration and Innovation in Teaching and Teacher Education Conference*, 14–16. http://www.mun.ca/edge2009/displaypapers.php (Accessed 15.11.09)

Guo, S. (2013). Economic integration of recent Chinese immigrants in Canada's second-tier cities: The triple glass effect and immigrants' downward social mobility. *Canadian Ethnic Studies*, *45*(3), 95–115. https://doi.org/10.1353/ces.2013.0047

Henley, D., & Young, J. (2009). Trading in education: The agreement on internal trade, labour mobility, and teacher certification in Canada. Canadian Journal of Educational Administration and Policy. *Canadian Journal of Educational Administration and Policy*, *91*. http://www.umanitoba.ca/publications/cjeap/articles/henleyyoung.html (Accessed 03.06.09)

Hilde, R. K., & Mills, A. (2015). Making critical sense of discriminatory practices in the Canadian workplace. *Critical Perspectives on International Business*, *11*(2), 173.

Hodkinson, H. (2009). Improving schoolteachers' workplace learning. In S. Gerwirtz, P. Mahony, I. Hextall, & A. Cribb (Eds.), *Changing teacher professionalism*. Routledge. https://doi.org/10.1080/02671520500077921

Holliday, A. (2005). *The Struggle to Teach English as an International Language*. Oxford University Press.

Holliday, A. (2006). Native-speakerism. *ELT Journal*, *60*(4), 385–387.

Jain, H. C., Horwitz, F., & Wilkin, C. L. (2012). Employment equity in Canada and South Africa: A comparative review. *The International Journal of Human Resource Management*, *23*(1), 1–17. https://doi.org/10.1080/09585192.2011.606115

Janusch, S. (2015). Voices Unheard: Stories of Immigrant Teachers in Alberta. *International Migration & Integration, 16*, 299–315.

Jenkins, J. (2000). *The Phonology of English as an International Language: New Models, New Norms, New Goals*. Oxford University Press. https://www.researchgate.net/publication/244511317_The_Phonology_of_English_as_an_International_Language

Kerekes, J. (2017). Language Preparation for Internationally Educated Professionals. In B. Vine (Ed.), *Routledge Handbook of Language in the Workplace*. Rutledge.

Kim, H. (2011). Native speakerism affecting nonnative English teachers' identity formation: A critical perspective. *English Teaching, 66*(4), 53–71.

Knight, P. T., & Trowler, P. R. (2010). Department-level cultures and the improvement of learning and teaching. *Studies in Higher Education, 25*(1), 69–83.

Kubota, R. (2001). Discursive construction of the images of US classrooms. *TESOL Quarterly, 35*(1), 9–37. https://doi-org.myaccess.library.utoronto.ca/10.2307/3587858

Liversage, A. (2009). Vital conjunctures, shifting horizons: High-skilled female immigrants looking for work", Work. *Employment & Society, Vol. 23 No. 1, pp. 120-141., 23*(1), 120–141. https://doi.org/10.1177/0950017008099781

Lopez, M. J. (2012). Skilled immigrant women in the US and the double earning penalty. *Feminist Economics, 18*(1), 99–134. https://doi.org/10.1080/13545701.2012.658429

Marom, L. (2017). Mapping the field: Examining the recertification of internationally educated teachers. *Canadian Journal of Education, 40*(3), 157–190.

Marom, L. (2019). From experienced teachers to newcomers to the profession: The capital conversion of internationally educated teachers in Canada. *Teaching and Teacher Education, 78*, 85–96.

Marom, L., & Ilieva, R. (2016). Becoming the "good teacher". In *Diversifying the teaching force in transnational contexts* (pp. 15–27). Sense Publishers.

Meares, C. (2010). A fine balance: Women, work and skilled migration. *Women's Studies International Forum, 33*(5), 473–481.

Medgyes, P. (1994). *The non-native teacher*. Macmillan.

Medgyes, P. (2000). Non-native speaker teacher. In M. Byram (Ed.), *Routledge encyclopedia of language teaching and learning* (pp. 444–446). Routledge.

Mezirow, J. (1978). Perspective transformation. *Adult Education, 28*(2), 100–110. https://doi.org/10.1177/074171367802800202

Mezirow, J. (2000). *Learning as Transformation: Critical Perspectives on a Theory in Progress*. ERIC.

Mezirow, J. (2003). Transformative Learning as Discourse. *Journal of Transformative Education, 1*(1), 58–63. https://doi.org/10.1177/1541344603252172

Mezirow, J. (2009). An overview on transformative learning. In K. Illeris (Ed.), *Contemporary theories of learning; Learning theorists...in their own words* (pp. 90–105).

Moussu, L. (2006). *Native and non-native English-speaking English as a second language teachers: Student attitudes, teacher self-perceptions, and intensive English program administrator beliefs and practices* [Purdue University]. https://files.eric.ed.gov/fulltext/ED492599.pdf

Moussu, L., & Llurda, E. (2008). Non-native English-speaking English language teachers: History and research. *Language Teaching, 41*(3), 315–348.

Mwebi, B. M., & Brigham, S. M. (2009). Preparing North American preservice teachers for global perspectives: An international teaching practicum experience in Africa. *Alberta Journal of Educational Research, 55*(3). https://doi.org/10.11575/ajer.v55i3.55336

Myles, J., Cheng, L., & Wang, H. (2006). Teaching in elementary school: Perceptions of foreign-trained teacher candidates on their teaching practicum. *Teaching and Teacher Education, 22*, 233–245.

Nazari, J. A., Herremans, I. M., Isaac, R. G., Manassian, A., & Kline, T. J. (2011). Organizational culture, climate and IC: an interaction analysis. *Journal of Intellectual Capital.* https://doi.org/10.1108/14691931111123403

Niyubahwe, A., Mukamurera, J., & Jutras, F. (2013). Professional integration of immigrant teachers in the school system: A literature review. *McGill Journal of Education, 48*(2), 279–296. https://doi.org/10.7202/1020972ar

Nowell, L. S., Norris, J. M., White, D. E., & Moules, N. J. (2017). Thematic analysis: Striving to meet the trustworthiness criteria. International. *Journal of Qualitative Methods, 16*(1), 1–13.

Oloo, J. A. (2012). Immigrant teachers in Saskatchewan schools: A human resource perspective. KEDI. *Journal of Educational Policy, 9*(2). https://www.researchgate.net/profile/James-Oloo/publication/234038059_Oloo_James_Alan_2012_Immigrant_teachers_in_Saskatchewan_schools_A_human_resource_perspective_KEDI_Journal_of_Educational_Policy_92_219-237/links/09e4150e7437a1a0e3000000/Oloo-James-Alan-2012-Immigrant-teachers-in-Saskatchewan-schools-A-human-resource-perspective-KEDI-Journal-of-Educational-Policy-92-219-237.pdf

Olsen, B. (2015). *Teaching What They Learn, Learning What They Live: How Teachers' Personal Histories Shape Their Professional Development.* Routledge.

Parkinson, P. (2008). Space for performing teacher identity: Through the lens of Kafka and Hegel. Teachers and Teaching: Theory and Practice. *Theory and Practice, 14*(1), 51–60.

Pendakur, K., & Pendakur, R. (2007). Minority Earnings Disparity Across the Distribution. *Canadian Public Policy, 33*(1), 41–60.

Pendakur, K., & Woodcock, S. (2010). Glass Ceilings and Glass Doors? Wage Disparity within and between Firms. *Journal of Business and Economic Statistics, 28*(1), 181–189.

Pennycook, A. (1994). *The Cultural Politics of English as an International Language*. Longman.

Pennycook, A. (2002). Mother tongues, governmentality, and protectionism. *International Journal of the Sociology of Language, 154*, 11–28.

Phillion, J. (2003). Obstacles to accessing the teaching profession for immigrant women. *Multicultural Education, 11*(1), 41–45.

Pollock, K. (2006). *Access to the teaching profession: Internationally educated teachers (IETs) experiences*. https://wall.oise.utoronto.ca/resources/Pollock_Internationally_Trained_Teachers_WALL2006.pdf

Pollock, K. (2015). The new" new teacher. In *The complexity of hiring, supporting, and retaining new teachers in Canada* (pp. 91–112). Canadian Association for Teacher Education/Canadian Society for Studies in Education.

Pollock, K. E. (2010). Transitioning to the teacher workforce: Internationally educated teachers (IETs) as occasional teachers. In *Challenging Transitions in Learning and Work* (pp. 165–182). Brill Sense.

Purkayastha, B. (2005). Skilled migration and cumulative disadvantage: The case of highly qualified Asian Indian immigrant women in the US. *Geoforum, 36*(2), 181–196.

Ramjattan, V. A. (2019). The white native speaker and inequality regimes in the private English language school. *Intercultural Education, 30*(2), 126–140.

Rudolph, N., Selvi, A. F., & Yazan, B. (2015). Conceptualizing and confronting inequity: Approaches within and new directions for the "NNEST movement." *Critical Inquiry in Language Studies, 12*(1), 27–50. https://doi.org/10.1080/15427587.2015.997650

Ryan, J., Pollock, K., & Antonelli, F. (2009). Teacher Diversity in Canada: Leaky Pipelines, Bottlenecks, and Glass Ceilings. *Canadian Journal of Education, 32*(3), 591–617.

Schmidt, C. (2010). Systemic Discrimination as a Barrier for Immigrant Teachers. *Diaspora, Indigenous, and Minority Education, 4*(4), 235–252. https://doi.org/10.1080/15595692.2010.513246

Schmidt, C., & Block, L. A. (2010). Without and within: The implications of employment and ethnocultural equity policies for internationally educated teachers. *Canadian Journal of Educational Administration and Policy, 100*. https://cjc-rcc.ucalgary.ca/index.php/cjeap/article/view/42785

Schmidt, C., & Gagné, A. (2015). Internationally educated teacher candidates in Canadian Faculties of Education: When diversity≠ equity. In *Handbook of Canadian research in initial teacher education* (pp. 295–311).

Schmidt, C., & Janusch, S. (2016). The Contributions of Internationally Educated Teachers in Canada: Reconciling What Counts with What Matters. In *Diversifying the Teaching Force in Transnational Contexts* (pp. 137–151). Brill Sense.

Schmidt, C., Young, J., & Mandzuk, D. (2010). The Integration of Immigrant Teachers in Manitoba, Canada: Critical Issues and Perspectives. *Journal of*

International Migration and Integration, *11*(4), 439–452. https://doi.org/10.1007/s12134-010-0149-1

Selvi, A. F. (2018). Myths and misconceptions about the NNEST movement and research. *The TESOL Encyclopedia of English Language Teaching*, *1*(8). http://nnestevo2014.pbworks.com/w/file/fetch/72049298/Selvi%20%28in%20press%29%20-%20Myths%20and%20Misconceptions%20about%20the%20NNEST%20Movement.pdf

Sfard, A., & Prusak, A. (2005). Telling identities: In search of an analytic tool for investigating learning as a culturally shaped activity. Educational Researcher. *Educational Researcher*, *34*(4), 14–22.

Shan, H., & Guo, S. (2013). Learning as sociocultural practice: Chinese immigrant professionals negotiating differences and identities in the Canadian labour market. *Comparative Education*, *49*(1), 28–41. https://doi.org/10.1080/03050068.2012.740218

Shervey, G., & O'Byrne, A. (2006). *Transitions to Alberta classrooms: A preparation program for teachers with international qualifications*. Alberta Education, Immigration and Integration (AEII).

Smith, T. M., & Ingersoll, R. M. (2004). What are the effects of induction and mentoring on beginning teacher turnover? *American Educational Research Journal*, *41*(3), 681–714.

Soheili-Mehr, A. H. (2018). *Immigrant Non-Native English Speaking Teachers in TESOL: The Negotiation of Professional Identities*. University of Toronto.

Tajeddin, Z., & Adeh, A. (2016). Native and nonnative English teachers' perceptions of their professional identity: Convergent or divergent? *Iranian Journal of Language Teaching Research*, *4*(3), 37–54.

Tang, C. (1997). The identity of the nonnative ESL teacher. *TESOL Quarterly*, *31*(3), 577–580.

Varghese, M., Morgan, B., Johnston, B., & Johnson, K. A. (2005). Theorizing Language Teacher Identity: Three Perspectives and Beyond. *Journal of Language, Identity & Education*, *4*(1), 21–44. https://doi.org/10.1207/s15327701jlie0401_2

Walsh, S. (2008). Listening to Difference in the Teaching of 'English': Insights from Internationally Educated Teachers. *Changing English*, *15*(4), 397–405. https://doi.org/10.1080/13586840802493043

Walsh, S. (2017). *Contemplative and artful openings: Researching women and teaching* (Vol. 1–193). Taylor & Francis.

Walsh, S., & Brigham, S. (2007). *Internationally educated teachers and teacher education programs in Canada*. Atlantic Metropolis Center. https://www.researchgate.net/profile/Susan-Walsh-14/publication/261794523_Internationally_educated_teachers_and_teacher_education_programs_in_Canada_Current_practices_Working_Paper_No_182-08_Atlantic_Metropolis_Centre/links/004635357c2605483b000000/Internationally-educated-teachers-and-teacher-education-programs-in-Canada-Current-practices-Working-Paper-No-18-2-08-Atlantic-Metropolis-Centre.pdf

Walsh, S. C., Brigham, S. M., & Wang, Y. (2011). Internationally educated female teachers in the neoliberal context: Their labour market and teacher certification experiences in Canada. *Teaching and Teacher Education, 27*, 657–665. https://doi.org/10.1016/j.tate.2010.11.004

Wenger, E. (1998). *Communities of practice: Learning, meaning, and identity*. Cambridge University Press.

White, C., & Ding, A. (2009). Identity and self in e-language teaching. In Z. Dörnyei & E. Ushioda (Eds.), *Motivation, Language Identity and the L2 Self* (pp. 333–349). Multilingual Matters. https://doi-org.myaccess.library.utoronto.ca/10.21832/9781847691293-018

Wimmer, R., Young, B., & Xiao, J. (2019). Innovating in the Margins of Teacher Education: Developing a Bridging Program for Internationally Educated Teachers. *In Education, 25*(2), 23–38.

Wong, L., & Wong, C. (2006). Chinese Engineers in Canada: A "Model Minority"? And Experiences and Perceptions of the Glass Ceiling. *Journal of Women and Minorities in Science and Engineering 12.4: 253-273.*, *12*(4), 253–273. https://doi.org/10.1615/JWomenMinorScienEng.v12.i4.10

Zhang, Y. (2016). Reviewing non-native English-speaking teachers' professional identity. *International Journal of Languages' Education, 1*(Volume 4 Issue 3), 320–320.

Zhao, K. (2012). *Internationally Educated Teachers in Canada: Transition, Integration, Stress, and Coping Strategies*. Ontario Institute for Studies in Education, University of Toronto.

JUSTINE JUN, PhD Candidate at OISE (Ontario Institute for Studies in Education), University of Toronto, is an English teacher educator and ESL/EAP instructor with long years of teaching experience in higher education in multiple countries. Her teaching, managing, and working experiences with migrant English instructors in Toronto led her to research on their workplace experiences. Her major research interests lie in the areas of English teacher education and support, intercultural and multicultural learning, English instructors' ongoing professional development, and higher education research. Email: justine.jun@mail.utoronto.ca.

Manuscript submitted: ***December 1, 2021***
Manuscript revised: ***April 7, 2022***
Accepted for publication: ***April 16, 2022***

Peer-Reviewed Article

© *Journal of Underrepresented and Minority Progress*
Volume 6, Issue 1 (2022), pp. 52-72
ISSN: 2574-3465 Print/ ISSN: 2574-3481 Online
http://ojed.org/jump

An Exploration of Black College Students' Conformity to Gender-Role Norms on Gender-Role Stress and Depression

April T. Berry
University of South Alabama, USA
Linda J.M. Holloway
Alabama State University, USA

ABSTRACT

Gender-role norms have caused men and women to be limited to many of the expectations that distinguish masculinity and femininity. Thus, the societally derived idea of what "makes a man a man" or a "woman a woman" has become the topic of gender-role conflict. Previous studies have investigated gender-role conflict between masculinity and femininity and gender-role norms, but there is a gap in understanding how conforming to gender-role norms affect mental health, particularly among Black cisgender college students. The present study examined the adherence to gender-role norms and its impact on gender-role stress and depression that results from conforming to traditional ideology in a sample of Black cisgender college students (n = 120). An Independent Samples T-Test revealed statistically significant differences between Black men's and women's conformity to gender-role norms and their reported experiences of gender-role stress, but not depression. Results suggest there are psychological consequences of conforming to traditional role norms for both Black male and female college students and could potentially impact how these students perceive their gender-roles in society.

Keywords: Black college students, conformity, depression, gender role norms, stress

INTRODUCTION

Gender-role norms limit women and men in their choices, behaviors, thoughts, and feelings. They provide guidance for women and men about what behavior is expected and accepted within a certain culture and what are off limits" (Mahalik et al., 2005, p. 5). People differ in their gender-role conformity to the extent that they "agree with or abide by the gender expectations set upon them by their culture" (Parent & Moradi, 2010, p. 97). Though there are many social explanations for why men and women conform to their gender-roles, there are health factors such as stress and depression that can be associated with such adherence (Mayor, 2015). However, research is limited in examining gender-role conformity in relation to mental health outcomes such as stress and depression, particularly among Black cisgender college students.

Today's gender-role norms are rooted in traditional roles that dominated the early and mid-20th century in the United States (Eagly et al., 2019). Such gender roles are entrenched in historic White, heterosexual, and Eurocentric worldviews and are based on a set of ideas about how society expects men and women to dress, behave, and present themselves (Blackstone, 2003). Thus, traditional masculinity ideology refers to men's acceptance and/or internalization of a culture's definition of masculinity and the specific beliefs that define the standards for male behaviors, such as the expectation that men are generally expected to be strong, aggressive, and bold (Levant et al., 1992; O'Neil, 1981; Pleck et al., 1993). In contrast, traditional femininity ideology is defined as individuals' beliefs about the appropriate roles and behaviors for women under patriarchy, such as the expectation for women to be polite, accommodating, and nurturing (Davis et al., 2018). Therefore, gender is often referred to as a social construct because of the attitudes, feelings, and behaviors that a given culture associates with a person's biological sex (American Psychological Association, 2012). Thus, this article will focus on the experiences of Black cisgender (e.g., a person's gender identity and gender expression align with their sex assigned at birth; APA, 2015) college students' gender-role conformity and experiences with stress and depression.

Specifically, Black men generally have endorsed traditional masculinity ideology to a stronger degree compared to White men (Levant et al., 2003; Levant et al., 1998; Pleck, 1994). Yet, other findings have shown no differences between Black men and White men in the endorsement of traditional masculinity ideology (Abreu et al., 2000). However, when comparing Black women and White women endorsement of traditional femininity ideology, results have shown that both groups endorse these gender-role norms to the same extent (Davis et al., 2018; Franklin, 1998). Such findings have been limited in nature and have not included examining these relationships particularly among Black college students.

Tinto (1993) suggested that college life is a time where development and identity formation occurs for students. His theory of persistence postulated that college students often separate from families to seek successful social and academic achievement. However, Black college students may often face difficulties with such adjustment and trying to adhere to role-norms they may have been socialized with in order to be accepted on their college campus (Sanchez et al., 1992). Additionally, Black male and female college students generally identify and cope with stressors differently (Greer et al., 2015; Hoggard et al., 2012; Negga et al., 2007). Black females are often engaged in internalizing behaviors such as depression and anxiety, whereas Black males are often engaged in externalizing behaviors such as substance use and violence (Hannon, 2016; Shahid et al., 2018).

Thus, gender-role conformity may have a direct bearing on health in both Black male and female college students (Flemming & Agnew-Brune, 2015; Mayor, 2015). Although society sets forth expectations that men and women must adhere to, it does not often consider the side effects of having to conform to standards set forth by others. Therefore, it is important to investigate what norms Black male and female college students are expected to conform to in order to guide further research and show how such role-norms play a vital role in susceptibility to negative health consequences, such as stress and depression.

CONFORMITY TO GENDER-ROLE NORMS

Gender-role norms are socially constructed norms that specify behaviors according to gender. "Social norms influence people to engage in specific social behavior, and gender role norms operate when people observe what most men or women do in social situations, are told what is acceptable or unacceptable behavior for men or women, and observe how popular men or women act. Thus, males and females come to learn what is expected of them when living their gendered lives" (Mahalik et al., 2005 p. 10). Conforming to gender-role norms can indeed cause psychological strain on men and women. The overall proposition of conformity is a concern for both social and clinical psychology, especially as it relates to socialization and the psychological consequences of stress and depression.

Mahalik (2005) found that sociocultural influences, especially those involving dominant or elite groups in a society, shape the expectations and standards related to gender-role identity. There are benefits and consequences to conforming to the role that identifies a man as a man and a woman as a woman. These underlying factors, however, show how those who are dominant shape and play a vital role in exacting those standards and guidelines that impact the roles of men and women (Flemming & Agnew-Brune, 2015).

In the psychology literature, the influence of male identity and socialization has often been posited as central to Black men's mental health, typically in negative ways (Wade & Rochlen, 2013). Researchers have suggested that Black men often negotiate their masculine identity within the context of a sociopolitical environment that may often relegate one's manhood to that of second-class status (i.e., masculinity becomes second in importance to a man's racial identity; Jones et al., 2018; Wade & Rochlen, 2013). Moreover, Black male college students have been found to depict their masculinity in what is known as "cool pose," which is characterized as a "ritualized form of masculinity that entails behaviors, scripts, physical posturing, impression management, and carefully crafted performances that deliver a single, critical message: pride, strength, and control" (Majors & Billson, 1992, p. 4). This often slightly contrasts with White college men's endorsement of masculinity. Masculine gender-role conformity generally from a Eurocentric perspective entails emotional control, winning, playboy attitudes, violence, self-reliance, risk-taking, power over women, dominance, primacy of work, pursuit of status, and disdain for LGBTQ+ individuals (Mahalik et al., 2005; Parent & Mordai, 2010; Ott, 2011). At this time, there is limited research that has examined the psychosocial correlates of Black male college students' conformity to gender-role norms and traditional masculinity ideology, specifically associated with their health-related attitudes and behaviors. However, endorsement of emotional control role-norms have been associated with less help-seeking intentions and less willing to forgive racially discriminatory experiences among Black college students (Fleming & Agnew-Brune, 2015; Hammond et al., 2006).

When exploring Black women's gender-role norms, research has shown that these roles have been profoundly impacted by the historical legacy of slavery and segregation (Davis et al., 2018). Economic forces, systemic oppression, and Black male incarceration and unemployment rates led Black women to compensate for the absence of men within family and community contexts by fulfilling both traditionally feminine and masculine gender-roles (Cole & Zucker, 2007; Collins, 2004). Although this gender-role flexibility began during slavery as way to manage work and family responsibilities, it continues to be adaptive for most Black women today to counter the experiences of poverty, racism, sexism, and oppression (Konrad & Harris, 2002). Although the traditional feminine role norms from a Eurocentric perspective includes niceness in relationships, thinness, modesty, domesticity, care for children, romantic relationships, sexual fidelity, and investment in appearance (Mahalik, 2005), Black women have also endorsed nontraditional gender roles that often put them at greater risk for experiences of stress (Littlefield, 2003). Thus, Black female college students may often experience gender-role conflict based on their previous socialization experiences that may lead to experiences of stress. This dilemma is often a result of Black female college students' perceptions of femininity that are often associated with role-norms.

From a social psychology perspective, adhering strictly to masculine and feminine norms can limit men's and women's potential by restricting the range of acceptable choices and behaviors available to them. In essence, masculine and feminine gender norms mirror and reinforce presumed gender differences that give greater value, power, and privilege to men and masculinity than to women and femininity. For example, while traditional feminine norms emphasize domesticity, the importance of a woman's appearance, and the use of cooperative or subordinate relational styles over more competitive ones (Mahalik et al., 2005), these imperatives are a stark contrast to traditional masculine aesthetics that emphasize worldliness, self-reliance, using violence to solve problems, and competitiveness. These gender-role norms create a dilemma for women because while women who uphold feminine norms may be compensated for satisfying this subordinate social role by being deemed to be appropriately feminine, this comes at the cost of not being able to express contrary or more traditionally masculine equivalents. Further, for those women who choose to violate traditional feminine norms in order to access the privileges usually reserved for men, they may achieve an elevated position in society, but it will likely come with disdain or censure in response to their mannish ways (Parent & Moradi, 2010)."

STRESS IN MEN AND WOMEN

The environment or society in which men and women live explain part of the gender-role norms that differentiates masculinity and femininity. However, when it comes to health-related factors such as stress, the influence of binary gender roles appear to affect men and women differently. Women experience more chronic stressors than men and consider stressors as more threatening; therefore, they will seek medical attention faster than men are likely to (Courtenay, 2000; Mayor, 2015; Saltonstall, 1993).

Stress triggers the hypothalamic-pituitary-adrenocortical axis and the sympathetic-adrenal medullar-axis, leading to the release of stress hormones such as cortisol and catecholamine. This generates dysfunctions of the immune system related to numerous diseases (Glaser & Kiecolt-Glaser, 2005; Lundberg, 2005; Cohen et al., 2007). Indeed, stress plays a vital role on one's overall health and well-being.

In addition, men and women are exposed to stressors that are differentiated based on gender-roles. Correlational research on the relationship between gender-roles and health has suggested that masculinity, in particular, is related to better physical and mental health (controlling for gender). Men who identify as masculine have better self-assessed general health, fewer physical symptoms, and better mental health; and they consult general practitioners less often (Mayor, 2015). Overall, the effect of masculinity on physical health is positive. From studies, traditional masculinity has been negatively associated with anxiety and depression, substance abuse, and antisocial behavior (Mayor, 2015). In contrast, traditional femininity has been correlated to high risks of depression and stress and has led to worse physical health outcomes (Hunt et al., 2007).

Although not much research has examined the psychological correlates of gender-role conformity and stress among Black male and female college students, stress may potentially play a role in gender differences that are expressed. Socialization has been related to the stress process, the experiences of stress, and the health of individuals (Mayor, 2015). Gender-role norms have implications for the way stressors are dealt with; nevertheless, it is important to access the impact gender-role norms have on stress and specifically how Black male and female college students respond to stressors.

DEPRESSION IN MEN AND WOMEN

Depression is one of the most common mental disorders and affects approximately 17 million people yearly in the United States alone (American Psychological Association, 2009). One of the most consistent psychiatric epidemiological findings is that depression is twice as common in women as in men (Magovcevic & Addis, 2008). Numerous theories have sought to explain women's vulnerability to depression (Cavanagh et al., 2017; Kessler, 2003; Noble, 2005). Data suggest, however, that this sex gap in depression may not be correlated with actual prevalence rates but instead, with factors such as men's unwillingness to seek help for depression and their tendency to underreport symptoms (Moller-Leimkuhler, 2002; Wilhelm et al., 2002).

To date, there has been limited research on "masculine or feminine" depression per se. However, in investigating prior research, it has been shown that men and women cope with depression differently. For example, men diagnosed with depression are more likely to engage in comorbid alcohol abuse problems, whereas women do not (Cochran & Rabinowitz, 2000; Fields & Cochran, 2011; Genuchi & Mitsunaga, 2015). This explains why men are more likely than women to participate in activities to avoid thinking about their depression. Women tend to admit they are experiencing depression and seek professional help, whereas men shun the idea of therapy.

Across the years, clinicians have proposed that men who adhere to traditional masculine norms are more likely to exhibit their depression in ways that align with those norms (Magovcevic & Addis, 2008; Mahalik et al., 2005; Parent & Moradi, 2010). Men tend to mask their depression by engaging themselves in behaviors such as drinking, using drugs, aggression, withdrawing from family or friends, reckless behavior, and over-focusing on work (Fields & Cochran, 2011). This potentially explains why some men and women become more socialized in their behavior in relation to their respective gender-roles.

Although there is a gap in the literature exploring Black male and female college students' adherence to gender-role norms and experiences of depression, it is important to grasp the concept that men and women are socialized to cope with depression differently, regardless of race (Beauboeuf-Lafontant, 2007; Hahm et al., 2015).

THE PRESENT STUDY

Previous studies have investigated traditional masculinity and femininity and gender-role norms, but there is a gap in understanding how conformity and adherence to such norms impacts overall mental health, particularly among Black college students. This study attempted to show that adherence to gender-roles explain part of why Black men and women experience psychological distress related to their role-norms.

Throughout their lives, Black men and women are taught (explicitly, implicitly, and vicariously) which behaviors are desirable for men and women in society (Mayor, 2015). Examples from Western culture include how Black women are expected to take care of the children; Black men are supposed to be the head of the household; Black women are to be reserved; and Black men are supposed to have power (Shahid et al., 2017). These gender-role traits have had an impact on Black men and women and have often led individuals to try to distinguish between what is right and what is not, based on gender. As has been suggested, this can lead to an increase in stressors that both Black men and women endure because of such expectations (Shahid et al., 2017).

To address the gaps in the literature, several hypotheses guided our analyses:

H_1: There will be a significant difference between Black male and female college students in conforming to gender-role norms

H_2: There will be a significant difference between Black male and female college students conforming to gender-role norms and gender-role stress

H_3: There will be a significant difference between Black male and female college students conforming to gender-role norms and depression.

RESEARCH METHOD
Participants and Procedures

Data were gathered through a convenient sample from a historically Black campus located in the Southeastern region of the United States. The students were randomly chosen from a male dorm and female dorm. The students were asked a specific question regarding their gender identity and biological sex to determine identification of *only* cisgender students. Additionally, there were also one undergraduate psychology course chosen at random that received extra credit points for participating in the study.

The sample demographics were fairly consistent with the general student groups in every area, except gender. For the present study, all participants self-identified as Black ($n = 120$). There were more males ($n = 70$) than females ($n = 50$). Most of the students classified themselves as undergraduate ($n = 118$). The majority of students reported their sexual orientation as heterosexual ($n = 115$).

Upon Institution Review Board (IRB) approval, participants were asked to complete an informed consent form and the surveys based on their gender identity (e.g., male or female). Participating students were able to receive an incentive of a care package that included a variety of snacks for their participation.

Measures

CMNI. The Conformity to Masculine Norms Inventory-46 (CMNI-46; Parent & Moradi, 2009) is often used to assess masculine gender-role conformity. It is a 46-item measure where items are rated on 4-point Likert Scale *(0-Strongly Disagree to 3-Strongly Agree),* where higher scores indicate more endorsement of that particular role norm. Nine masculine role norms are assessed in this measure: Winning (e.g., "In general, I will do anything to win"), Emotional Control (e.g., "I tend to keep my feelings to myself"), Primacy of Work (e.g., "My work is the most important part of my life"), Risk-Taking (e.g., "I frequently put myself in risky situations"), Violence (e.g., "Sometimes violent action is necessary"), Heterosexual Self-Presentation (e.g., "I would be furious if someone thought I was gay"), Playboy (e.g., "If I could, I would frequently change sexual partners"), Self-Reliance (e.g., "I hate asking for help"), and Power over Women (e.g., "In general, I control the women in my life"). An examination of the Masculinity Norms subscales revealed that there is strong support for validity (Parent & Moradi, 2009). Evidence has shown that the subscales differentiated men from women and men who engaged in high-risk behaviors from those who did not. Additionally, there is strong convergent and concurrent validity. To compare reliability and validity with other masculine inventories, Mahalik et al. (2005) used the Brannon Masculinity Scale Short Form (BMS; Brannon & Juni, 1984), the Male Role Norms Inventory (MRNI; Levant et al., 1992), and the Gender-Based Attitudes toward Marital Roles Scale (GBATMR; Hoffman & Kloska, 1995). Using a Pearson Correlation, the results indicated that the CMNI-46 scores were significantly correlated with scores from the BMS, MRNI, and the GBATMR.

CFNI. The Conformity to Feminine Role Norms Inventory (CFNI; Mahalik et al., 2005) is a measure that was designed to assess women's conformity to a variety of feminine role norms found within the dominant culture in the United States. It is an 84-item measure where items are rated on 4-point Likert Scale *(0-Strongly Disagree to 3-Strongly Agree)*, where higher scores indicate more endorsement of that particular role norm. Eight feminine role norms are assessed in this measure: Nice in Relationships (e.g., "It is important to let people know they are special"), Involved with Children (e.g., "I would baby-sit for fun"), Thinness (e.g., I would be happier if I was thinner"), Sexual Fidelity (e.g., "I would feel extremely ashamed if I had many sexual partners"), Modesty (e.g., I feel uncomfortable being singled out for praise"), Involved in Romantic Relationship (e.g., "When I am in a romantic relationship, I give it all my energy"), Domestic (e.g., "It is important to keep your living space clean"), and Investment in Appearance (e.g., "I spend more than 30 minutes a day doing my hair and make-up"). This measure scale has shown high internal consistency estimates and test/retest reliability over a period of 2 to 3 weeks (Mahalik et al., 2005).

AMGRSS. The Abbreviated Masculine Gender Role Stress Scale (AMGRSS; Swartout et al., 2015) is a 15-item scale, shortened from the original 40-item scale that assesses men's masculine gender role stress. Items are rated on a 6-point Likert scale *(1-Not at all stressful to 6-Extremely Stressful)*. Sample items include rating one's level of gender-role stress as it relates to: "Being outperformed at work by a woman," and "Having your children see you cry." Likert Scale Item Response Theory has shown that the abbreviated scale has held promise of capturing the same information as the full 40-item scale. Relative to the 40-item scale, the total score of the abbreviated scale has demonstrated comparable convergent validity and shown reliability in various domains such as masculine identity, trait anger, alcohol involvement, and anger expression (Swartout et al., 2015). Higher scores indicate more masculine gender role stress.

FGRS. The Feminine Gender Role Stress Scale (FGRS; Romero, 2008) is a 39-item scale, proven to exhibit high reliability and construct validity that assesses the cognitive tendency to appraise threats and challenges to femininity as stressful. Items are rated on a 6-point *(1-Not at all stressful to 6-Extremely Stressful)*. The dimensions assessed within this measure include: Fear of Unemotional Relationships, Fear of Physical Unattractiveness, Fear of Victimization, Fear of Behaving Assertively, and Fear of Not Being Nurturant. Sample items include rating one's level of stress as it relates to: "Being perceived by others as overweight," and "Having to deal with unwanted sexual advances." The Cronbach's coefficients of each of these five factors indicates good internal consistency, and the test-retest reliability over a two-week period is .82 (Romero, 2008). Higher scores indicate more feminine gender role stress.

BDI-II. The Beck Depression Inventory-II (BDI-II; Beck et al., 1996) is a one of the most widely known scales. It has been reported highly reliable in any given population. It consists of 21 items that contains four self-evaluative statements scored on a Likert scale from 0 to 3. Participants are asked to report their experiences of each item experienced during the past two weeks. Responses are summed, ranging from 0 to 63, with higher scores indicating more depressive symptoms. Regarding construct validity, the BDI-II can show differences between those who are depressed and those who are not. Test-retest reliability has been studied and has shown consistency within weeks apart. This scale also has high construct and convergent validity. The BDI-II has been given to outpatients in clinical settings and has shown accurate measurements for symptoms for depression. Factorial validity has also been established by the inter-correlation of the responses to the 21-items (Dozois et al., 1998).

Analysis Plan

Before analyzing data from the quantitative surveys, the data was screened on the univariate and multivariate levels. Additionally, descriptive statistics were calculated for the dataset. This included gender, age, and sexual orientation. Data were screened for individuals who failed to complete the requirements of the study (e.g., identifying as a Black cisgender college student). Only participants who completed at least 80% of each measure were examined. The primary analysis considered of an Independent Samples T-Test to compare the means between the two unrelated groups (e.g., Black males and Black females) on the same continuous dependent variables (e.g., stress and depression). First, we ensured that the stress and depression dependent variables could be measured on a continuous scale. Second, we ensured that the gender-role conformity independent variable consisted of two categorical independent groups (e.g., Black males and Black females). Next, we checked for independence of observations to determine no relationship between the observations in each group or between the groups themselves. As an important assumption, this was done to ensure that there were different participants in each group with no participant being in both the Black male or Black female group. Then, we checked to ensure there were no significant outliers. Finally, we checked for normality and homogeneity of variance to ensure the data were normally distributed for both Black males and Black females and that both the comparison groups had the same variance.

RESULTS
Preliminary Analyses

Prior to conducting our main analyses, we screened data for missing values, univariate and multivariate outliers, and violations of normality. Missing values, univariate outliers, and multivariate outliers were minimal (i.e., less than 2% of the total sample).

Primary Analyses

To test the hypothesis that there would be a significant difference between Black male and female college students in conforming to gender-role norms, an independent samples t-test was performed. As can be seen in Table 1, this hypothesis was supported. The assumption of homogeneity of variances was tested and satisfied via Levene's F test, $F(118) = 1.30, p = .26$. The independent samples t-test was associated with a statistically significant effect $t(118) = -5.21, p = .000**$. Thus, it can be concluded that there is a statistically significant difference between Black male and female college students' conformity to gender-role norms and that Black female college students are conforming more to their gender-role norms compared to Black male college students based on the Mean for both conditions. Cohen's d was estimated to be 0.9, which is a large effect size based on Cohen's (1992) guidelines. Group statistics are reported in Table 1.2.

Table 1
Conformity to Gender-Roles Among Black Male and Female College Students

	F	Sig	T	df	p	MD	SED	95% Confidence Interval of the Difference	
								Lower	Upper
Equal variances assumed	1.30	.26	-5.21	118	.000**	-13.47	2.59	-18.59	8.35
Equal variances not assumed			-5.30	111	.000**	-13.47	2.54	-18.51	-8.43

Note. F= Levene's F Test; Sig= Significance of F Test; T= T-Test; df= Degrees of Freedom; MD = Mean Difference; SED= Standard Error of Difference. *** $p < .001$.

Table 1.2
Conformity to Gender-Roles Group Statistics

Cisgender	N	M	SD	SEM
Male	70	42.83	14.51	1.73
Female	50	56.30	13.14	1.86

Note. N = Number in Sample; M= Mean; SD = Standard Deviation; SEM = Standard Error of the Mean.

To test the hypothesis that there would be a significant difference between Black male and female college students' conformity to gender-role norms and stress, another independent samples t-test was performed. As can be seen in Table 2, this hypothesis was supported. The assumption of homogeneity of variances was tested and satisfied via Levene's F test, $F(118) = 3.59$, $p = .06$. The independent samples t-test was associated with a statistically significant effect $t(118) = -6.79$, $p = .000**$. Thus, it can be concluded that there is a statistically significant difference between Black male and female college students' conformity to gender-role norms and reported levels of stress. Specifically, Black female college students are conforming more to their gender-role norms and reporting significantly higher levels of stress compared to Black male college students based on the Mean for both conditions. Cohen's d was estimated to be 1.28, which is a large effect size based on Cohen's (1992) guidelines. Group statistics are reported in Table 2.2.

Table 2

Gender-Role Stress Among Black Male and Female College Students

	F	Sig	T	df	p	MD	SED	95% Confidence Interval of the Difference	
								Lower	Upper
Equal variances assumed	3.59	.06	-6.79	118	.000**	-6.38	.94	-8.24	-4.52
Equal variances not assumed			-7.08	117	.000**	-6.38	.91	-8.16	-4.59

Note. F= Levene's F Test; Sig= Significance of F Test; T= T-Test; df= Degrees of Freedom; MD = Mean Difference; SED= Standard Error of Difference. *** p <.001.

Table 2.2

Gender-Role Stress Group Statistics

Cisgender	N	M	SD	SEM
Male	70	58.34	5.54	.66
Female	50	64.72	4.32	.61

Note. N = Number in Sample; M= Mean; SD = Standard Deviation; SEM = Standard Error of the Mean.

Finally, to test the hypothesis that there would be a significant difference among both Black male and female college students' conformity to gender-role norms and depression, a final independent samples t-test was performed. As can be seen in Table 3, this hypothesis was not supported. The assumption of homogeneity of variances was tested and satisfied via Levene's F test, $F(118) = .59, p = .45$. The independent samples t-test was associated with a statistically significant effect $t(118) = -1.07, p = .29$. Thus, it can be concluded that there is not a statistically significant difference between Black male and female college students' conformity to gender- norms and reports of depression. The scores among Black male college students do not vary too much more than the scores for Black female college students. Cohen's d was estimated to be 0.2, which is a small effect size based on Cohen's (1992) guidelines. Group statistics are reported in Table 3.2.

Table 3

Gender-Role Stress Among Black Male and Female College Students

	F	Sig	T	df	p	MD	SED	95% Confidence Interval of the Difference	
Equal variances assumed	.59	.45	-1.07	118	.29	-2.04	1.91	Lower -5.81	Upper -1.73
Equal variances not assumed			-1.12	117	.27	-2.04	1.83	Lower -5.66	Upper 1.58

Note. F= Levene's F Test; Sig= Significance of F Test; T= T-Test; df= Degrees of Freedom; MD = Mean Difference; SED= Standard Error of Difference. *** $p < .001$.

Table 3.2

Depression Group Statistics

Cisgender	N	M	SD	SEM
Male	70	12.40	11.27	1.35
Female	50	14.44	8.71	1.23

Note. N = Number in Sample; M= Mean; SD = Standard Deviation; SEM = Standard Error of the Mean.

DISCUSSION AND CONCLUSIONS

This study explored Black male and female college students' conformity to gender-role norms and its impact on gender-role stress and depression. The findings supported Hypothesis I in large part and indicated that there is a statistically significant difference between Black male and female college students' conformity to gender-role norms, and Black female college students are conforming more to their gender-role norms compared to Black male college students. Hypothesis II was also supported, resulting in a statistically significant difference between Black male and female college students' conformity to gender-role norms and levels of gender-role stress. Finally, Hypothesis III was not supported because there was no statistically significant difference between Black male and female college students' conformity to gender-role norms and reports of depression, particularly in this sample.

The results of this study suggest that Black female college students are striving to meet the expectations and standards set forth by their gender-roles and are experiencing feminine gender-role stress. Instead of seeking help, most Black female college students suffer in silence in attempts to meet the expectations of others while maintaining the façade of strength, determination, and resilience (Abrams et al., 2014; Jones & Shorter-Gooden, 2003; author's name removed for blind-review, 2019). This is known as the conflict between traditional femininity ideology and the Strong Black Woman ideology (Davis et al., 2018). The Strong Black Woman Ideology is specific to Black women's adherence to both traditional (e.g., caretaking) and nontraditional (e.g., independence/self-reliance) feminine norms, which is expected to be associated with stressful experiences. Thus, a potential reason this sample of Black female college students are endorsing more conformity to gender-role norms and experiences of stress is due to striving for femininity from a traditional perspective as well as a nontraditional one.

Additionally, Black male college students are also reporting conforming to gender-role norms and experiences of stress, although to a lesser degree compared to Black female college students. Such findings are consistent with the literature related to gender-role conflict that Black men often experience (Wade & Rochlen, 2013). Black men often experience competing masculinities-one culture of masculinity from a Eurocentric perspective and the other from a more Afrocentric perspective (Wade, 1996; Wester, 2008). Such findings do support the relationships between gender-role conformity and psychological distress in Black men (Carter et al., 2005; Wester et al., 2006). Sources of such relationships are related to the obstacles of racism and discrimination that inhibit Black men's fulfillment of male role expectations, thus resulting in reported levels of stress (Wade & Rochlen, 2013).

Therefore, this study's implications include the need for an intervention to help both Black male and female college students feel free to express their perceptions of masculinity and femininity both in a traditional or nontraditional sense without being impacted psychologically. Both Black male and female college students experience a "double-edged sword effect," where they want to be accepted within the dominant society (e.g., endorsement of traditional roles), while also wanting to be a part of their own cultural group (e.g., endorsement of nontraditional roles). Thus, such gender-role conflict can result in psychological consequences. Based on research conducted by Kundu and Cummins (2013), results suggest that students are often conforming particularly on college campuses due to the need for affiliation, accuracy, and a positive self-concept. Therefore, it is crucially important for counselors, therapists, and the campus community to create a campus climate that allows for students to feel accepted, validated, and respected for endorsing their perspective gender-role norms and perceptions of masculinity and femininity without feeling marginalized or alienated for doing so. Moreover, researchers should explore ways to prevent or reduce stress from occurring when college students may feel like they cannot meet the demands of society. It is acceptable for students to choose opposite from others and not feel as if they have done wrong or chosen incorrectly, yet they chose what they felt was right. Such decisions can impact overall psychological well-being.

Limitations and Conclusions

The present findings should be interpreted with respect to some key limitations. First, the measures administered were self-report in nature, thus administering observational measures would lend to more complete and unbiased data. Second, this study was correlational and was conducted at a single point in time. Thus, it does not allow causal conclusions about the temporal order of these variables. Third, this study was conducted at a single institution in the Southeastern region of the United States with only Black male and female participants. Thus, the results may vary in different contexts or in more diverse samples of college students. Fourth, this study only used an independent samples *t*-test for analysis to determine significant differences between males and females in relation to experiences of stress and depression rather than more advanced statistical analyses such as Structural Equation Modeling to determine the direct relationships of these constructs. Finally, research has previously shown that the measures administered in this study were normed, standardized, and used primarily on European males and females. Although this study may contribute to the literature by examining these concepts in a primarily Black sample, these instruments are limited in research involving more diverse samples.

In conclusion, the findings of this study indicate the need for an intervention to help both Black males and females understand the importance of being themselves in the midst of what society says is appropriate by gender. When studying conformity, it is clearly shown that individuals submit to pressure when authority is in control (Kundu & Cummins, 2013). Thus, it is important in the field of psychology that we continue to discuss the concept of *liberation* and empower our young Black men and women to embrace their gender-roles and not submit themselves to White, Eurocentric values and norms. Although White, Eurocentric values and norms are considered "the standard," Black values and norms are also equally important to explore and potentially adhere to. Future studies should seek to incorporate a more thorough understanding of Afrocentric values and norms and explore if adherence to such norms impact experiences with stress and depression among Black cisgender male and female college students.

REFERENCES

Abrams, J. A., Maxwell, M., Pope, M., & Belgrave, F. Z. (2014). Carrying the world with the grace of a lady and the grit of a warrior: Deepening our understanding of the "Strong Black Woman" schema. *Psychology of Women Quarterly, 38*, 503-518. https://doi.org/10.1177%2F0361684314541418

American Psychological Association (2009). *Depression Resource Guide.*

American Psychological Association. (2012). Guidelines for psychological practice with lesbian, gay, and bisexual clients. *American Psychologist, 67*(1), 10–42. https://doi.org/10.1037/a0024659

American Psychological Association. (2015). Guidelines for psychological practice with transgender and gender nonconforming people. *American Psychologist, 70*(9), 832-864. http://dx.doi.org/10.1037/a0039906

Barry, H., Bacon, M. K., & Child, I. L. (1957). A cross-cultural survey of same sex. *Abnormal and Social Psychology, 55,* 327-332. https://doi.org/10.1037/h0041178

Beck, A. T., Steer, R. A., & Brown, G. K. (1996). *Manual for the Beck Depression Inventory-II.* San Antonio, TX: Psychological Corporation.

Beauboeuf-Lafontant, T. (2007). You have to show strength: An exploration of gender, race, and depression. *Gender & Society, 21*(1), 28-51. https://doi.org/10.1177/0891243206294108

Bem, D. J. (1972). Self-perception theory. *Advances in Experimental Social Psychology.* New York: Academic Press.

Bem, S. (1981). Gender schema theory: A cognitive account of sex typing. *Psychological Review, 88*(4), 354-364. https://doi.org/10.1037/0033-295X.88.4.354

Bern, D. J., & Allen, A. (1974). On predicting some of the people some of the time: The search for cross-situational consistencies in behavior. *Psychological Review, 81,* 506-520. https://doi.org/10.1037//h0037130

Berns, S., Capra, C. M., Moore, S., & Noussair, C. (2010). Neural mechanisms of the influence of popularity on adolescent ratings of music. *Neuroimage, 49,* 2687-2696. https://doi.org/10.1016/j.neuroimage.2009.10.070

Blackstone, A. M. (2003). Gender roles and society. In Julia R. Miller, Richard M. Lerner, & Lawrence B. Schiamberg (Eds)., *Human Ecology: An Encyclopedia of Children, Families, Communities, and Environments* (pp. 335-338). Santa Barbara, CA.

Brannon, R., & Juni, S. (1984). A scale for measuring attitudes about masculinity. *Psychological Documents, 14*, 6–7.

Cavanagh, A., Wilson, C. J., Kavanagh, D. J., & Caputi, P. (2017). Differences in the expression of symptoms in men versus women with depression: A systematic review and meta-analysis. *Harvard Review of Psychiatry, 25*(1), 29-38. https://doi.org/10.1097/HRP.0000000000000128

Cochran, S., & Rabinowitz, F. (2000). *Men and depression: Clinical and empirical perspectives.* San Deigo, CA: Academic Press.

Cohen, J. (1992). A power primer. *Psychological Bulletin, 112*(1), 155-159. https://doi.org/10.1037/0033-2909.112.1.155

Cohen, S., Janicki-Deverts, D., & Miller, G. E. (2007). Psychological stress and disease. *JAMA, 298,* 1685-1687. https://doi.org/10.1001/jama.298.14.1685

Cole, E. R., & Zucker, A. N. (2007). Black and White women's perspectives on femininity. *Cultural Diversity & Ethnic Minority Psychology, 13,* 1-9. https://doi.org/10.1037/1099-9809.13.1.1

Collins, P. H. (2004). *Black sexual politics: African Americans, gender and the new racism.* New York, NY: Routledge.

Courtenay, W. H. (2000). Constructions of masculinity and their influence on men's well-being: A theory of gender and health. *Social Science and Medicine, 50*(10), 1385-1401. https://doi.org/10.1016/s0277-9536(99)00390-1

Davis, A. W., Levant, R. F., & Pryor, S. (2018). Traditional femininity versus strong Black women ideologies and stress among Black women. *Journal of Black Studies, 49*(8), 820–841. https://doi.org/10.1177/0021934718799016

Dozois, D. J. A., Dobson, K. S., & Ahnberg, J. L. (1998). A psychometric evaluation of the Beck Depression Inventory-II. *Psychological Assessment, 10,* 83-89. https://doi.org/10.1037/1040-3590.10.2.83

Eagly, A. H., Nater, C., Miller, D. I., Kaufmann, M., & Sczesny, S. (2019). Gender stereotypes have changed: A cross-temporal meta-analysis of U.S. public opinion polls from 1946 to 2018. *American Psychologist.* Advance online publication. http://dx.doi.org/10.1037/amp0000494

Fields, A. J., & Cochran, S. (2011). Men and depression: Current perspectives for health care professionals. *American Journal of Lifestyle Medicine, 5,* 92-100. https://doi.org/10.1177%2F1559827610378347

Fleming, P. J., & Agnew-Brune, C. (2015). Current trends in the study of gender norms and health Behaviors. *Current opinion in psychology, 5,* 72–77. https://doi.org/10.1016/j.copsyc.2015.05.001

Franklin, A. J. (1998). Invisibility syndrome in psychotherapy with African American males. In R. L. Jones (Ed.), *African American mental health* (pp. 395–413). Hampton, VA: Cobb & Henry Publishers.

Genuchi, M. C., & Mitsunaga, L. K. (2015). Sex differences in masculine depression: Externalizing symptoms as a primary feature of depression in men. *The Journal of Men's Studies, 23*(3), 243–251. https://doi.org/10.1177/1060826514561986

Glaser, R., & Kiecolt-Glaser, J. K. (2005). Stress induced immune dysfunction: Implications for health. *Nature Reviews Immunology, 5,* 243-251. https://doi.org/10.1007/S11199-013-0315-y

Greer, T. M., Ricks, J., & Baylor, A. A. (2015). The moderating role of coping strategies in understanding the effects of intragroup race-related stressors on academic performance and overall levels of perceived stress for African American students. *Journal of Black Psychology, 41*(6), 565–585. https://doi.org/10.1177/0095798414560018

Hahm, H. C., Cook, B. L., Ault-Brutus, A., & Alegria, M. (2015). Intersection of race-ethnicity and gender in depression care: Screening, access, and minimally adequate treatment. *Psychiatric services, 66,* 258-264. https://doi.org/10.1176/appi.ps.201400116

Hannon, C. R. (2016). *Stress, coping, and well-being of African American college women: A grounded theory study.* Dissertation.

Hoffman, L. W., & Kloska, D. D. (1995). Parents' gender-based attitudes toward marital roles and child-rearing: Development and validation of new measures. *Sex Roles, 32,* 273–295. https://doi.org/10.1007/ BF01544598

Hoggard, L., Byrd, C., & Sellers, R. (2012). Comparison of African American college students' coping with racially and nonracially stressful events. *Cultural Diversity & Ethnic Minority Psychology,* 18, 329-339. https:// doi.org/10.1037/a0029437

Holloway, L. J. M. (2019). Ain't nobody blues like a Black woman's blues. *EC Psychology and Psychiatry, 8.8.*

Hunt, K., Lewars, H., Emslie, C., & Batty, G. D. (2007). Decreased risk of death from coronary heart disease amongst men with higher 'femininity' scores: a general population cohort study. *International Journal of. Epidemiology, 36,* 612-620. https://doi.org/10.1093/ije/dym022.

Jones, C., & Shorter-Gooden, K. (2003). *Shifting: The double lives of Black women in America.* New York, NY: Harper Collins.

Jones, M. K., Buque, M., & Miville, M. L. (2018). African American gender roles: A content analysis of empirical research from 1981 to 2017. *Journal of Black Psychology, 44*(5), 450–486. https:// doi.org/10.1177/0095798418783561

Kessler, R. C. (2003). Epidemiology of women and depression. *Journal of Affective Disorders, 74*(1), 5-13. https://doi.org/10.1016/S0165-0327(02)00426-3

Konrad, A. M., & Harris, C. (2002). Desirability of the Bem Sex-Role Inventory items for women and men: A comparison between African Americans and European Americans. *Sex Roles, 47,* 259-271. https:// doi.org/10.1023/A:1021386727269

Kundu, P., & Cummins, D. D. (2013). Morality and conformity: The Asch Paradigm applied to moral decisions. *Social influence, 8*(4), 268-279. https://psycnet.apa.org/doi/10.1080/15534510.2012.727767

Levant, R. F., Hirsh, L., Celantano, E., Cozza, T., Hill, S., MacEcheron, M., & Schnedeker, J. (1992). The male role: An investigation of contemporary norms. *Journal of Mental Health Counseling, 14*, 325–337.

Levant, R. F., Majors, R. G., & Kelley, M. (1998). Masculinity ideology among young African American and European American women and men in different regions of the United States. *Cultural Diversity and Mental Health, 4*, 227–236. https://doi.org/10.1037/1099-9809.4.3.227

Levant, R. F., Richmond, K., Majors, R. G., Inclan, J. E., Rossello, J. M., Heesacker, M., . . . Sellers, A. (2003). A multicultural investigation of masculinity ideology and alexithymia. *Psychology of Men & Masculinity, 4*, 91–99. https://doi.org/10.1037/1524-9220.4.2.91

Littlefield, M. B. (2003). A womanist perspective for social work with African American women. *Social Thought, 22*(4), 3-17. https://doi.org/10.1080/15426432.2003.9960354

Lundberg, U. (2005). Stress hormones in health and illness: the role of work and gender. *Psychoneurendocrinology, 30*, 1017-1021. https://doi.org/10.1016/j.psyneuen.2005.03.014

Magovcevic, M., and Addis, M. E. (2008). The Masculine Depression Scale: Development and psychometric evaluation. *Psychology of Men & Masculinity, 9*(3), 117-132. https://doi.org/10.1037/1524-9220.9.3.117.

Mahalik, J. R., Locke, B. D., Ludlow, L. H., Deimer, M. A., Scott, R. P., Gottfriend, M., et al. (2005). Development of the Conformity to Masculine Norms Inventory. *Psychology of Men & Masculinity, 4*, 3-25. https://psycnet.apa.org/doi/10.1037/1524-9220.4.1.3

Mahalik, J. R., Morray, E. B., Coonerty-Femiano, A., Ludlow, L. H., Slattery, S. M., & Smiler, A. (2005). Development of the Conformity to Feminine Norms Inventory. *Sex Roles, 52*, 417-434. https://psycnet.apa.org/doi/10.1007/s11199-005-3709-7

Mayor, E. (2015). Gender roles and traits in stress and health. *Frontiers in Psychology, 6*, 779. https://doi.org/10.3389/fpsyg.2015.00779.

Moller-Leimkuhler A. (2002). Barriers to help-seeking by men: A review of sociocultural and clinical literature with particular reference to depression. *Journal of Affective Disorders, 71*, 1–9. https://doi.org/10.1016/s0165-0327(01)00379-2

Negga, F., Applewhite, S., & Livingston, I. (2007). African American college students and stress: school racial composition, self-esteem and social support. *College Student Journal, 41*(4), 823-826.

Neisser, U. (1976). *Cognition and reality*. San Francisco: Freeman.

Noble, R.E. (2005). Depression in women. *Metabolism, 54*(5), 49-52. doi: https://doi.org/10.1016/j.metabol.2005.01.014

O'Neil, J. M. (1981). Male sex role conflicts, sexism, and masculinity: Psychological implications for men, women, and the counseling psychologist. *The Counseling Psychologist, 9*, 61–80. https://doi.org/10.1177/ 001100008100900213

Ott, R. (2011). *White Male College Students: An Examination of Identity Development, Masculinity, and Institutional Connections*. Dissertation.

Parent, M. C., & Moradi, B. (2010). Confirmatory factor analysis of the Conformity to Feminine Norms Inventory. *Sex Roles, 52,* 417-435. https://doi.org/10.1111/j.1471-6402.2009.01545.x

Pleck, J. H., Sonenstein, F. L., & Ku, L. C. (1993). Masculinity ideology and its correlates. In S. Oskamp & M. Constanza (Eds.), *Gender issues on contemporary society* (pp. 85–110). Newbury Park, CA: Sage.

Pleck, J. H., Sonenstein, F. L., & Ku, L. C. (1994). Attitudes toward male roles: A discriminant validity analysis. *Sex Roles, 30,* 481–501. https://doi.org/10.1007/BF01420798

Romero, N. (2008). Femininity, feminine gender role stress, body dissatisfaction, and their relationships to bulimia nervosa and binge Eating Disorder (Master's Thesis). Retrieved from Virginia Polytechnic Institute and State University Library.

Saltonstall, R. (1993). Healthy bodies, social bodies: Men's and women's concepts and practices of health in every life. *Social Science Medical, 36*(1), 7-14. https://doi.org/10.1016/0277-9536(93)90300-S

Sanchez, J. E., Marder, F., Berry, R., & Ross, H. (1992). Dropping out: Hispanic students, attrition, and the family. *College and University, 67*(2), 145–150.

Shahid, N. N., Nelson, T., & Cardemil, E. V. (2018). Lift every voice: Exploring the stressors and coping mechanisms of Black college women attending predominantly White institutions. *Journal of Black Psychology, 44*(1), 3–24. https://doi.org/10.1177/0095798417732415

Swartout, K. M., Parrott, D. J., Cohn, A. M., Hagman, B. T., & Gallagher, K. E. (2015). Development of the Abbreviated Masculine Gender Role Stress Scale. *Psychology Assessment, 27*(2), 489-500. https://doi.org/ 10.1186/1471-2458-9-21.

Tinto, V. (1993). *Leaving college: Rethinking the causes and cures of student attrition.* Chicago, IL: University of Chicago Press.

Wade, J. C. (2009). Traditional masculinity and African American men's health related attitudes and behaviors. *American Journal of Men's Health, 3,* 165–172. https://doi.org/10.1177/1557988308320180

Wester, S. R., Vogel, D. L., Wei, M., & McLain, R. (2006). African American men, gender role conflict, and psychological distress: The role of racial identity. *Journal of Counseling & Development, 84,* 419–429. https://doi.org/10.1002/j.1556- 6678.2006.tb00426.x

Wester, S. R. (2008). Male gender role conflict and multiculturalism: Implications for counseling psychology. *The Counseling Psychologist, 36,* 294–324. https://doi.org/10.1177/0011000006286341

Wilhelm, K., Roy, K., Mitchell, P., Brownhill, S., & Parker, G. (2002). Gender differences in depression risk and coping factors in a clinical sample. *Acta Psychiatrica Scandinavica, 106,* 45–53. https://doi.org/10.1034/j.1600-0447.2002.02094.x

April T. Berry, MS, is a Doctoral Candidate at the University of South Alabama and a Psychology Intern at the University of Florida's Counseling and Wellness Center. Her major research interests lie in the area of diversity, equity, and inclusion efforts on a college campus and within the broader world, social justice advocacy, racial and gender socialization experiences among people of color, and coping with oppressive systems (i.e., discrimination/racism). Email: ab1724@jagmail.southalabama.edu.

Linda J.M. Holloway, Ed.D., NCC, is an Associate Professor and Program Coordinator for the master's in counseling Programs at Alabama State University. Her major research interests lie in the area of Black women and their mental wellness, career counseling, social justice advocacy, and cultural literacy among young children. Email: lholloway@alasu.edu.

Manuscript submitted: ***November 11, 2021***
Manuscript revised: ***March 7, 2022***
Accepted for publication: ***April 16, 2022***

Peer-Reviewed Article

© *Journal of Underrepresented and Minority Progress*
Volume 6, Issue 1 (2022), pp. 73-96
ISSN: 2574-3465 Print/ ISSN: 2574-3481 Online
http://ojed.org/jump

Work-Life Management Challenges for Graduate Students of Color at an HBCU During a Pandemic

Sharlene Allen Milton
Nia Caldwell
Deval Popat
Tavril Prout
Morgan State University, USA
Cherese Godwin
Temple University, USA

ABSTRACT

This article expands the student work-life discussion to include nontraditional graduate students of color. The Afrocentric theory is used as a conceptual framework. A collaborative inquiry approach was used to capture the reflections and experiences of three urban graduate students of color matriculating at a historically Black university during a pandemic. Six themes emerged: COVID-19, ties that bind, financial responsibility, linked fate, mental and physical well being, and student work-life management. The article concludes with implications for education, research, and policy.

Keywords: Collaborative inquiry, graduate students of color, work-life balance, work-life management

INTRODUCTION

According to Okahana and colleagues (2020), 24.8% of graduate students enrolled in the Fall 2019 semester in the United States were students of color, of which 0.50% were American Indian/Alaska Native, 12.10% Black/African American, 0.20% were Native Hawaiian/Other Pacific Islander, and 11.90% were Latinx individuals. Graduate students of color are often married or single with dependents, dependent on student aid for financial resources, and in need of emotional support and paid work, whether part-time or full-time (National Center for Education Statistics, n.d.). As these students of color seek upward mobility via higher education, they often experience distance from their communities and have to redefine themselves socially to find support (Holley & Gardner, 2012; Walsh et al., 2021). Common student work-life issues, such as addressing financial and caretaking responsibilities and taking on student loan debt, are often eclipsed by curriculum and other graduate program requirements, leaving some urban nontraditional graduate students of color feeling invisible and unsupported by their new academic community (Brus, 2006; Choy, 2002; National Center for Education Statistics, n.d.). Graduate students who are parents report higher levels of stress related to work-family balance, as well as a general lack of support from university systems (Dolson & Deemer, 2020; Springer et al., 2009; Theisen et al., 2018).

Many nontraditional graduate students of color or those who are married, parents, caretakers, reliant upon full-time or part-time work, or rely on loans to pay for school, are often unprepared for the initial cerebral jolt that accompanies student work-life management issues and, specifically, the increase in stress associated with working, parenting, and meeting the academic demands of graduate school (Lin, 2016). Adjustments associated with the COVID-19 crisis added another layer of stress. The student work-life stressors for graduate students of color while experiencing a pandemic include increased caretaking responsibilities for children while working from home (Nodine et al., 2021), facing disproportionate deaths of loved ones as a result of COVID-19 (Fortuna et al., 2020), navigating feelings of discrimination, whether personally or vicariously (Campbell & Valera, 2020; Dolson & Deemer, 2020), safeguarding mental health (Chirikov et al., 2020), and meeting the demands of graduate school remotely.

Existing literature that specifically highlights the student work-life experiences of graduate students of color during a pandemic is limited (Walsh et al., 2021; Wan Mohd Yunus et al., 2021). This article expands the student work-life discussion to include nontraditional graduate students of color. Afrocentric theory is used as a conceptual framework. This article emerges from a collaborative inquiry approach to capture the reflections and experiences of three urban graduate students matriculating at a Historically Black College or University (HBCU) during a pandemic, thus adding voice on the discussion of student work-life for graduate students of color. The article concludes with implications for education, research, and policy.

LITERATURE REVIEW
Community as Culture

Afrocentric theory focuses on the epistemology of people within the African diaspora (i.e., Black and people of African descent, such African American, Afro-Caribbean, and Afro-Latino) and places them at the center of analysis (Asante, 2003; Schiele, 1996). Using a Black person as the center of analysis, Boyd-Franklin (1989) discussed seven levels to describe the interdependent and multisystemic levels of Black families: "individual, subsystems, family household, extended family, nonblood kin and friends, church and community resources, social services agencies and other outside systems" (p. 150). Cultural values such as communalism, interconnectedness, and spirituality had their genesis in West Africa (Bent-Goodley, 2003; Martin & Martin, 2002; McPhatter, 2016; Schiele, 1996), have survived the great Maafa (i.e., the middle passage or transatlantic slave trade; Ani, 1994), and are currently practiced among many individuals of African descent.

For many people of African descent, the interlinking of community is also psychologically, emotionally, and spiritually expressed through linked fate. Linked fate is associated with a keen sense of identification and consciousness that occurs in a given community will impact an individual of that community (Dawson, 1994; Gay & Tate, 1998; Jaynes & Williams, 1989; Simien, 2005). For people of African descent, linked fate is also associated with an extensive history of lived experiences of discrimination, oppression, systemic racism, disparities, and inequities, especially in the United States (National Urban League, 2020; Simien, 2005). This "stage of identification, whereby individuals come to see themselves as sharing a linked fate with other African American people, leads to collective action as a necessary form of resistance" (Simien, 2005, p. 530). Community serves as the ties that bind (Butler, 1992), a protective factor for many individuals of African descent, inclusive of historically Black colleges and universities and the many Black undergraduate and graduate students.

Work-Life Balance

The topic of balancing work and personal life falls into multiple typologies: work-family conflict, work-family integration, and work-life balance (Alleman et al., 2018). Work-life balance has been defined in a variety of ways. The most widely used definition is that work-life balance is "an overall appraisal of the extent to which individuals' effectiveness and satisfaction in work and family roles are consistent with their life values at a given point in time" (Greenhaus & Allen, 2011, p. 80). Alleman and colleagues (2018) assert that work-life balance holds three primary assumptions:

> 1) Family is a woman's responsibility and work is a man's responsibility; 2) with the increase in workplace policies addressing time flexibility, individuals can choose the way in which they engage in work; and 3) the work-life balance discussion primarily focuses on a Western Anglo-American world view and neglects the worldview of non-western cultures (p. 80).

As more parents of color seek graduate education (Council of Graduate Schools, 2018), there is a need to expand the traditional view of women being nurturers to include women as providers (Littlefield, 2003).

Student Work-Life Balance

Discussion of the effects of work and life for the matriculating student has only recently begun, particularly for urban graduate students of color. From 1986 to 2004, there was an increase in the number of full-time matriculating students at 4-year universities working at least 20 hours per week (Fox et al., 2005). Specifically, in 2000, 77% of full-time matriculating students were working at least 27 hours per week (Butler, 2007). As of 2011, 82% of graduate students worked full-time (Davis, 2012). The student work-life balance literature highlights challenges and stressors, the importance of social support, practical solutions, and suggestions for the academic world (Evans et al., 2018; King and Herb, 2012).

To examine the challenges of work-life balance for women and to recognize the increased stressors with which women contend, McCutcheon and Morrison (2018) conducted a qualitative research study of 65 academic women, 32 faculty and 33 graduate students. The researchers identified three themes: masculine workplace norms, consequences of work-life balance, and choosing between work and family. Many of the participants indicated that they had to choose between academics, work, and family. One stated, "For women especially, it is difficult to even consider having a family while pursuing higher education. One should not have to choose between an academic career and having children" (McCutcheon &

Morrison, 2018, p. 241). This study also highlighted how graduate students encounter work-family conflict. One participant stated:
> I do feel as if my dissertation has suffered because I had a child. I feel torn between the two, and have chosen to prioritize my child over my writing. . . . It is taking me longer to finish and I worry about time-to-completion. . . . After a full day of clinical work, spending time with my child, and household chores, I am too tired to write at night. (McCutcheon & Morrison, 2018, p. 244)

This study demonstrates that male-focused workplace cultures and the demands of academia may increase the likelihood that mothers feel like they have to choose between work, family, and pursuing their academic goals.

Wyland et al. (2013) examined the relationship between nonwork demands (i.e., school involvement) and school-work conflict and investigated the mediating effects of school-work conflict on the relation between school involvement and job performance. Wyland and colleagues (2013) used the Grzywacz and Marks's (2000) scale of work-family conflict to measure school-work conflict, and the Karasek's (1979) scale was used to assess school involvement. In the first round of surveys distributed to 339 graduate business students enrolled at a large Midwestern university, there were 171 usable responses. Based on hierarchical regression analyses, school involvement significantly and positively predicted school-work conflict. The second round involved paper-based surveys for the same population, with 54 usable responses, and incorporated supervisor-rated measures of job performance (i.e., job dedication, task performance, and interpersonal facilitation). Hierarchical regression analyses showed that schoolwork conflict negatively predicted job dedication and interpersonal facilitation and predicted task performance. Researchers also found that school-work conflict fully mediated the relation between school involvement and job dedication and task performance. The findings suggest that the level of involvement in graduate school (which may involve registering for classes, going to school meetings, participating in group projects, and applying for and participating in grant fellowships) impacts work role, work responsibilities, and interpersonal work relationships, increasing school-work conflict for the student and possibly increasing levels of stress (Wyland et al., 2013).

Stress and Mental Health

The overlapping roles of provider, nurturer, and student can prove stressful to graduate students. El-Ghoroury and colleagues (2012) examined academic stressors and coping strategies for 273 psychology graduate students. When listing stressors, more than half the sample identified academic responsibilities, finances/debt, anxiety, and poor work/school-life balance. Further, a quarter of the student participants listed an additional eight challenges: burnout/compassion fatigue; death, loss, or grief; depression; family issues; marital/relationship issues or other interpersonal issues; physical health issues; professional isolation/lack of social support; and research responsibilities (El-Ghoroury et al., 2012). Many participants reported that incorporating self-care activities such as exercising, social support, or mental health breaks helped decrease added stressors of work-life balance (El-Ghoroury et al., 2012).

In an extensive literature review on barriers and challenges of nontraditional students, Lin (2016) found that students' multiple roles lead to increased time constraints and conflicts to work and life, which create increased levels of stress and anxiety and lead to a decrease in self-confidence. Evans and colleagues (2018) surveyed 2,279 graduate students representing 26 nations and 234 institutions, with 56% studying in the humanities or social sciences and 38% studying in the biological and physical science fields. The survey, which included validated clinical scales for anxiety and depression, was distributed to students via email and social media. Among the graduate students, 41% had moderate to severe anxiety based on the GAD07 scale, compared to 6% of the general population. Additionally, 39% of participants had moderate to severe depression, compared with 6% of the general population. Among the women, 40% had anxiety and 41% were depressed, compared with 34% and 35% of men, respectively. A total of 56% of graduate students who experienced moderate to severe anxiety and 55% of those who reported depression did not agree with the statement that their "work-life balance was good." Positive support from advisors positively impacted students' emotional well-being.

Researchers have begun to examine work-life balance in two contexts specific to the current study: COVID-19 and graduate students of color. Chirikov and colleagues (2020) conducted a 3-month study on the impact of the COVID-19 pandemic on the mental health of undergraduate and graduate students at research universities. Of the 15,346 graduate and professional students surveyed, 32% screened positive for major depressive disorder and 39% screened positive for generalized anxiety disorder based on clinically validated screening tools. Increased rates of major depressive and generalized anxiety disorders were higher among students from lower economic status, students of color, women, and students who are caregivers.

Walsh and colleagues (2021) conducted five online focus groups during the COVID-19 pandemic, with participants including five doctoral students of color, six master's students of color, seven faculty, six administrators (inclusive of administrative faculty), and six family members associated with the doctoral students of color. Following a reflexive thematic analysis approach (Braun & Clarke, 2006), four major themes emerged: (1) resources and access to them, (2) adjustments to home and family life, (3) magnification of existing nonfinancial issues, and (4) fear of and possibilities for the future. All participants reported a lack of distinction between work-life and home-life challenges. One family member commented that it was as if "there's no balance at all." A master's student indicated that some professors "upped our assignments, because we are at home," which contributed to a lack of balance. Working from home without a dedicated workspace or ability to study at the school or the library created challenges, as did the need to obtain supplies and set up a home office. A faculty member commented that many faculty "don't understand how the intersection of mental health, identity, and systemic oppression really play a role in being able to actually finish [a graduate degree]" (p. 966). When considering fears for the future, one participant expressed concern for her parents and the lack of ability to fly home. Recommendations included mental health check-ins for family; resource guides, inclusive of ethnic resource guides; race-based support; and faculty support in managing the anxiety with student-family demands in the face of COVID-19 (Walsh et al., 2021).

Support

Wilks (2008) examined the relationship between academic stress, social support, and resilience among 314 social work students, 144 at the bachelor's level and 170 at the master's level. Wilks (2008) reported several demands leading to academic stress: "course requirements; time management issues; financial burdens; interactions with faculty; personal goals; social activities; adjustment to the campus environment; and lack of support networks" (p. 106). Academic stress was moderately lowered when the support of family or friends was present throughout the student's tenure. Additionally, this social support added to students' resilience (Wilks, 2008). The study concluded that gaining social support from friends, family, professors, and internship staff is crucial because it fosters resilience and lifelong relationships that can help an individual professionally and personally.

Other researchers have also found that academic stress can be decreased when supportive services and networks are provided (El-Ghoroury et al., 2012; Evans et al., 2018; Walsh et al., 2021; Wyland et al., 2013). Social support may be experienced through various persons, such as friends, strangers, partners, family, and community members, as well as institutions. Social support has a direct impact on students' overall well-being—emotionally, physically, and mentally—by reducing stress, anxiety, and depression (Brus, 2006; Lin, 2016; Taylor, 2010; Wilks, 2008).

Graduate student life is challenging on its own, and adding work and life to the mix can exacerbate challenges. King and Herb (2012) suggested that planning break times and providing rewards can have a positive effect on an individual's emotional well-being. "For example, some students choose a time in the evening when they will stop working on any research or class activities. During this time, they refrain from checking university email, creating class lectures, reading articles for class, and browsing Google Scholar" (p. 125). King and Herb (2012) suggested that graduate students make physical and social health a priority and immerse themselves in their community. Alleman and colleagues (2018) also suggested prioritizing one's spiritual, mental, and physical health to achieve better work-life balance. Evans and colleagues (2018) suggested that graduate students should have enhanced access to mental health services, and academia should prioritize mental health resources.

CONCEPTUAL FRAMEWORK
Afrocentric Perspective

The Afrocentric perspective provides a way of finding understanding, a community, and an inclusive pedagogy. Founded in the social reality of the Black experience of people of African descent living in the diaspora, the Afrocentric perspective aims to counter the deficit-based, dysfunctional narrative of African American people and those of African descent (Asante, 2003; Schiele, 1996, 2010). Contrary to Eurocentric thought, the Afrocentric perspective "solidly place[s] the study of people of African descent within African cultural values and worldviews" (McPhatter, 2018, p. 5). Afrocentric thought is an alternative social science epistemology reflecting the cultural and political realities of African American people rather than dominant Eurocentric-based paradigms. This African-centered thought seeks to remove dysfunctional notions and damaging theoretical and practice approaches toward people of African descent and validates a worldview that is indigenous to this group. The Afrocentric perspective seeks to transform human and society holistically, that is, spiritually, morally, and humanistically (Schiele, 1996).

According to Bent-Goodley (2005), seven principles best describe an Afrocentric worldview. *Fundamental goodness* is the view that individuals are inherently good. *Self-knowledge* involves being consciously self-aware of strengths and needed improvements when interacting with others. *Communalism* highlights honoring the interdependence of individuals and concerns of the group before self. *Interconnectedness* relates to the collective plight of disparity, racism, and exploitation, as well as working in tandem for the health and well-being of all. *Spirituality* focuses on acknowledging the existence of God. *Self-reliance* involves gaining skill sets and a knowledge base that allow for contributions that will benefit the collective. *Language and oral tradition* acknowledge the multiple modes of communication including, but not limited to, words, music, songs, proverbs, dance, community gatherings, and dialects.

Bent-Goodley's (2005) principles are fundamental to not only the Black culture but extends to the culture of many HBCUs. Historically Black Colleges and Universities are often viewed as institutions that provide an opportunity for ethnic identification while meeting the exclusive educational, and sociocultural needs of its majority African American student populations in a nurturing manner (Darrell, Littlefield, Washington, 2016).

RESEARCH METHOD

Just as the Afrocentric paradigm is an inclusive pedagogy that places the individual of study in the center for the purpose of understanding and removes pathology-based practices (Schiele, 1996,), so too does inquiry-based learning (Bray et al., 2000).

> "Within new paradigm research, collaborative inquiry (CI) is used as an umbrella term to encompass genres of research that are participatory, democratic and reflective in design, method and dissemination (Bridges & MCGee 2011, p. 211)."

As part of the current study, we sought to capture the reflections and experiences of three urban graduate students matriculating at an HBCU during a pandemic. Participants engaged in personal and collaborative episodes of reflection answering four questions: (a) What was your experience like as a graduate school student at an HBCU? (b) How did you experience support while in graduate school? (c) What were some of your stressors as a graduate student? (d) How did you experience student work-life management as a graduate student? Questions were constructed based upon a review of the current literature, including student work-life balance, academic stress, and social support (El-Ghoroury et al., 2012; Evans et al., 2018; Walsh et al., 2021; Wilks, 2008; Wyland et al., 2013).

Participants

As part of the current study, the authors reflected on their student work-life balance while attending graduate school during a pandemic. Specifically, a convenience sample was used, as the participants of the current project served as authors, as they were experts in telling their own stories. All three participants were self-identified students of color enrolled full-time or part-time in a Master of Social Work program at an HBCU. All the students engaged in caretaking responsibilities. "Jay" is a 25-year-old African American single woman born in America who works as a part-time graduate assistant and a part-time childcare worker. At times, she was the caretaker for her three cousins. A full-time student, she was in the final year of her master's in social work program. "Dee" is a 43-year-old Asian single woman born in India. She works as an adjunct informational technology instructor, with 12 years of experience in that field. She is the caretaker for her father. A part-time student, she recently completed the second year of her master's program. "El" is an American-born 30-year-old African American man with one child. He is employed as a law enforcement officer and family services caseworker. He was enrolled part-time and recently completed the first year of the master's program.

Materials

Materials used for this collaborative inquiry were interview questions that were derived from the literature (El-Ghoroury et al., 2012; Evans et al., 2018; Walsh et al., 2021; Wilks, 2008; Wyland et al., 2013). The questionnaire allowed for the ability to acquire descriptive data, to explore perceptions of work-life balance of graduate students of color while experiencing a pandemic. Multiple group sessions occurred remotely, where participants engaged in storytelling and reflective analogy as they answered each question. Participants also used journaling as a means to capture personal reflections which allowed for meaning making at the individual a group level.

Design

We used inquiry learning, which is a powerful, democratic, equitable, and robust way of facilitating adult learning experiences that are potentially transformational to the individuals involved (Bray et al., 2000; Brooks & Watkins, 1994; Kasl & Yorks, 2010). Bray and colleagues (2000) posited that collaborative inquiry rests on an evolving paradigm of inquiry that celebrates participation and democracy, where participants are co-inquirers. Collaborative inquiry "is a process consisting of repeated episodes of reflection and action through which a group of peers strives to answer a question(s) of importance to them" (Bray et al., 2000, p. 6). The process involves four stages: framing the problem, collecting evidence, analyzing evidence and documents, and sharing and celebrating. The framing of the problem by the facilitator aids the group in finding its focus. In collecting evidence, the facilitator guides the group in developing shared understandings and building additional knowledge. The facilitator analyzes evidence to assist the group in identifying patterns and themes and forming conclusions. In the final stage, the facilitator guides students to document, share, and celebrate their new understandings (Donohoo, 2013, p. 5). As part of the current study, we used various components of the collaborative inquiry process to extend our understanding. The process included four phases as represented in Collaborative Inquiry in Practice (Bray et al., 2000): Phase 1: Forming, Phase 2: Creating, Phase 3: Acting, Phase 4: Making Meaning.

The group formed as a result of a desire to capture the reflections and experiences of three urban graduate students matriculating at a Historically Black College or University (HBCU) during a pandemic. Once the group was formed rules of engagement were established. It was determined that meetings would occur weekly, and we would remain in contact via bi-weekly conference calls and e-mail. Literature was reviewed and interview questions were made. As we seamlessly approached the acting phase of our inquiry, we met and participated in storytelling to better share our overall experiences. Discussions were led by a Caribbean-American, female facilitator who is an assistant professor of social work at an HBCU and a licensed clinical social worker.

We used narrative analysis (Reissman, 2008) and Saldana's (2009) method to code data surrounding the work-life balance of three graduate students of color. Reflections were categorized into themes and subthemes with guidance from the facilitator and were analyzed during a collective meaning-making session by all participants. Quotations were selected based on which narrative reflection identified the theme's most salient points. A manual process was used to cluster and thematize the reflections.

To increase trustworthiness, the study used thick, rich description, saturation, and member checking (Saladana, 2009). Thick, rich descriptions were captured during personal and collaborative reflections. The three co-inquirers performed member checking. Over the course of three sessions, they assisted with coding the data and asking challenging questions. Seidman (2006) posited that saturation of information refers to a point where new knowledge is no longer being revealed. Saturation was achieved during the last collaborative reflective discussion.

RESULTS

Six themes emerged from the study: COVID-19, ties that bind, financial responsibility, linked fate, mental and physical well-being, and student work-life management.

COVID-19

The COVID-19 pandemic affected students' school/work-life balance through loss, grief, and cancellation of major life events, all while they had to navigate the terrain of remote instruction. "Jay" reported:

> My grandfather passed away, graduation was canceled, trips were canceled, and that was all due to COVID-19. So not only did I have to balance work and life, but now I had to learn how to survive in the online world.

Additionally, the transition to remote work and education provided opportunities to focus time on graduate studies and family. "El" shared:

> COVID-19 provided me an opportunity for continuing graduate education, which became a number one focus. COVID-19 minimized travel to work and school, which increased time and focus on academic studies, in addition to home schooling of my young son. As a nontraditional graduate student, the conversion to full telework status of my two full-time employment positions allowed an increase in overall work productivity. COVID-19 has provided un-normal opportunities of self-education, creativeness, autonomy, independence, and the development of new skills such as personal accountability, time management, personal efficiency, and nontraditional use of technology (Zoom and Google Meet) outside of the office and classroom.

Living through a pandemic while attending graduated school was viewed as survival as the students managed the disappointment of not experiencing the coveted graduation ceremony, managing the grief of the loss of loved ones due to Covid-19, as well as adjusting to remote instruction. On the other hand, another graduate student of color experienced an increase in both caretaking responsibilities, productivity and student work-life management strategies.

Ties That Bind

"Jay," "Dee," and "El" discussed and reflected on the importance of various support systems as they completed coursework. "Dee":

> One of my teachers told me my first year that "you need to build a net of support so when you fall they can catch you." Social support systems were so crucial in matriculating through my program. I was blessed to have many opportunities that provided support during my first year. I was selected in a fellowship for my first year, which . . . provided a support system, accountability, and mentorship from the lead professors, which was needed to successfully balance the work, school, and life.

"Dee" viewed support systems as family (immediate or extended), obliging colleagues, supervisor, and mentor. She likened support systems to mile markers that aid in the success of student work-life management.

> In my family, I have two married sisters and parents as well as a big extended family. A marathon serves an analogy for my systems of support. At certain mile markers, in order to be successful, I have time-management skills; healthy support system; helpful colleagues; a successful game plan; access to physical and psychological therapy; having an inspiring supervisor and mentor.

Various types of social support were deemed essential and offered accountability, mentorship,

Financial Responsibility

"Jay," "Dee," and "El" discussed and reflected on how they were unable to solely focus on school since they had to meet financial obligations. "Dee" explained best:

> As a nontraditional student, I do not have the luxury of just focusing solely on school. I had to juggle three part-time jobs, not by choice, all while balancing my school schedule, internship, and schoolwork.

For "Jay," "Dee," and "El," work prevented them from focusing on their studies exclusively. Paid employment was a necessity for as they were primarily responsible to pay for school and meet additional fiscal demands.

Linked Fate

In discussing stress related to student work-life, "Jay," "Dee," and "El" reflected on the personal, cognitive, and emotional traumatic effects of linked fate as related to racism in the form of police brutality. "Dee" reported, "As an African American student, I also had to deal with the retraumatization of racism because of police brutality which led to the deaths of George Floyd, Brionna Taylor, and many more." "El" stated:

> I was very saddened by the racism and police brutality that has occurred in our nation for the last 300-plus years. Before police brutality it was discrimination, Jim Crow laws, lynchings, hangings, and the mutilation of slaves. All of those themes have snowballed into police brutality. . . . So being an African American male, I have to look over my shoulders twice or even three times before making any move or making a decision. My face is always in my rearview mirror while operating my personal vehicle and government vehicle. For me, it has been an integral part of my career and personal life on how to proceed with law enforcement, when I get pulled over, making sure I have my credentials on me at all times, placing my badge and license outside of the window, with both of my hands, so they know that I am law enforcement and I have in my possession a firearm and/or to reduce anxiety and fear when approaching the unknown vehicle. So there are a lot of procedures that I have to take in order to maintain my personal safety.

Seeing or hearing about the senseless deaths of African American men and women as result of racism and police brutality via social media was traumatizing and negatively impacted student work-life management. Additionally, personal cautionary procedures were put in place when stopped law enforcement to avoid ensure personal safety. Although these acts of racism and brutality were experienced by individuals unknown to the graduate students of color, there was vicarious impact because of a communal sense of belonging to the Black community along with knowledge of systemic, oppressive, discriminatory, and brutal acts inflicted upon individuals of African descent living in America.

Mental and Physical Well-Being

Being conscious of mental and physical well-being and prioritizing self-care were discussed by "Dee," "Jay," and "El" as ways to manage the stress associated with student work-life balance. "Dee" reported, "I realized the importance of prioritizing my mental health and implementing self-care activities throughout the program."
"Jay" commented:

> Apart from friends and family, I resort to meditation and yoga to relieve anxiety occurring from tight deadlines and expectations to perform better. Eating healthy food is another way to support my physical and mental health. What is stressful is consistently performing 3.0 or above

grade-point average, paying tuition on time, socializing with family and friends, dealing with anxiety and sometimes depression while comparing yourself to others.

"Dee," "Jay," and "El" were cognizant of how much they could withstand or limiting what they took on as a way to keep stress in check. "El" reported:

Mental health and physical health are two important components as it relates to graduate studies. Taking two classes allows me to maintain my mental and physical health. I have been pursuing this master's in social worker degree for a while. Therefore, I know what comes along with pursuing the degree, which alleviates the stress. It's important to know what people can and cannot take on.

Being aware of stress and personal stress limitations was important to the management of student work-life management. Self-care strategies that aided in stress reduction were important in supporting physical health and decreasing mental health challenges, such as anxiety and coping with depression.

Student Work-Life Management

"Dee," "Jay," and "El" reported that student work-life management was not easy and required the implementation of various strategies with support systems at the core. "Dee compared the totality of the student work-life experience to a rite of passage.

I figured it was going to be easy to balance graduate school, work, and life, but I soon realized that this was going to be a challenge. Balancing work, school, and life requires a vast amount of strategies to help mitigate or alleviate the burden, but creating a supportive environment is crucial. When I entered graduate school, I was a child; when I graduated I became an adult. It was like a rite of passage.

"Jay" reported using time management as an additional strategy to achieve student work-life harmony.

Having previous IT work experience and attending conferences on effective time management helped with managing time and organizing my daily/monthly/yearly activities. Student work-life harmony for me means assignment and paper due dates are met; GPA of 3.0 or above is maintained; happy family and friends gathering; sparing time for self on the weekend; getting positive feedback from my supervisor at work; opportunity to make new friends while cherishing old ones; no financial, psychological, or physical stress; at the end of year personal and professional goals are achieved.

DISCUSSION AND CONCLUSIONS

During this collaborative inquiry, the nontraditional graduate students of color were the center of analysis, inclusive of the interconnected multisystem (Boyd-Franklin, 1989) around their lives (Asante, 2003; Schiele, 1996). All of the graduate students of color valued the importance of functioning in multiple roles, especially the roles of worker, caretaker, and student. "Dee," "Jay," and "El" worked and engaged in caretaking roles for a child, parent, or extended family.

The impact of the COVID-19 pandemic on student work-life management was twofold for "Dee," "Jay," and "El." "Dee" and "Jay" experienced grief and loss associated with the death of family members, not being able to see family members and friends, transitioning from attending classes in person to adjusting to remote education, and not being able to engage in major life events such as graduation. "El" viewed the teleworking and stay-at-home order as an opportunity to spend quality time with his child and give concentrated attention to graduate school, resulting in increased productivity.

Support systems, whether immediate family, extended family, friends, colleagues, professors, or mentors, allowed for interrelations that created a community for "Dee," "Jay," and "El," replicating cultural values associated with people of color (Bent-Goodley, 2003, 2005; Martin & Martin, 2002; McPhatter, 2016; Schiele, 1996; Wilks, 2008). The various support system typologies as posited by Taylor (2010) were also experienced by "Dee," "Jay," and "El." Informational support in the form of a fellowship along with conferences that focused on time management offered guidance and information on how to cope with the stressors of student work-life management. Although "Dee," "Jay," and "El" offered instrumental support, such as the caretaking of family members, they also received the same support when needed. Validation evident in emotional support was experienced through the fellowship, friends, professors, colleagues, supervisor, and mentor (Taylor, 2010).

Stressors associated with student work-life management were offset by the communalism associated with the various types of support systems for "Dee," "Jay," and "El." Gaining social support from friends, family, professors, and internship staff was crucial in the graduate school experience, because it fostered community interconnectedness in the form of linked fate (Bent-Goodley, 2003, 2005; Simien, 2005). As "Dee" expressed, the accountability and interconnectedness associated with being psychologically and emotionally linked with others was essential to the success of student work-life management. On the other hand, racism in the form of police brutality was widely publicized via various social media outlets; as such, linked fate was also experienced, wherein "Dee" and "El" were vicariously affected, whether in the form of trauma or hypervigilance (Bent-Goodley, 2005; Schiele, 1996; Simien, 2005). Stressors were also offset by strategies of organization and time management (King & Herb, 2012), self-care activities, and mental and physical health strategies (Alleman et al., 2018; Bent-Goodley, 2005; El-Ghoroury et al., 2012; Wilks, 2008; Wyland et al., 2013).

The Greenhaus and Allen (2011) definition of work-life balance appeared insufficient for the participants, as various components of student work and life were in constant flux, creating stress and tension. Coping with living in a pandemic, dealing with the negative psychological and cognitive effects associated with linked fate, meeting academic and work demands, and managing the various subgroups along multisystemic levels of community on a daily basis requires a myriad of individuals and support systems to meet the academic, work, or life goals of "Dee," "Jay," and "El."

Limitations

Several limitations to the current study are relevant. First, the authors were participants in the study, which provided a limited view on the subject matter. Secondly, the participants were sampled from a single university program at a single point in time. Further, participants were familiar with each other prior to data collection, so it is possible they may have not wanted to share specific personal challenges or experiences. Furthermore, the graduate students of color of this inquiry experience had privileges that do not necessarily apply to other people of color in nonacademic settings. All of the graduate students of color involved in this collaborative inquiry were college educated, had support networks, and were knowledgeable of self-care strategies to assist them with their student work-life management challenges where other people of in nonacademic settings may not have availability to these resources. The method and sample size was small which provided a narrow view on the subject as well as an inability to replicate.

IMPLICATIONS

The results of this study have implications for education, policy, and research. "Dee" and "El discussed the importance of teachable moments from faculty or mentors that they recalled during the pandemic. Due to the decrease of the face-to-face interaction associated with a traditional graduate school experience, professors and students need to increase the level of involvement to ensure success for the urban graduate student of color. Both faculty and students should be knowledgeable about available resources inclusive of general, ethnic, and cultural supportive services. Additionally, information about student issues, guidelines for accessing appropriate support, and strategies for identifying students who struggle to achieve work-life balance (Brus, 2006).

Brus (2006) also suggested that for universities to provide appropriate support, student affairs should gather three types of information about graduate students:

> (1) basic demographic information; (2) identification of types of academic support the student is interested in, such as study groups, tutoring services, job shadowing opportunities, and cooperative childcare networks; and (3) a checklist of cultural, spiritual, recreational, intellectual, and political interests and activities they are interested in (p. 6).

Parenting status should also be included as basic demographic questions for all universities and colleges.

Additionally, as suggested by "Dee," graduate students should be offered workshops and peer mentorship programming specifically geared to student work-life management, allowing for education, resource linkage, verbal processing, and emotional support. Graduate programs should provide opportunities for fellowship programs for first-year students to increase support, accountability, and mentorship. Programs for recent alumni to volunteer to mentor first-year graduate students could also provide mentorship and guidance. Further, second-year students could create committees in areas such as mental health or stress strategies to support first-year students.

Regarding policy, "Dee," "El" and "Jay" discussed the importance of mental health. Mental health counseling should be required for graduate students. Evans and colleagues (2018) suggested that graduate students should have enhanced access to mental health services, and policies should be created that prioritize mental health resources in academia. In agreement with the recommendations of Alleman and colleagues (2018), graduate students need to prioritize their spiritual, mental, and physical health.

Furthermore, for graduate students of color who are parents, policies are needed that allow for no-cost or low-cost childcare or collaborations with reputable childcare providers. Additionally, as individuals continue to experience economic hardship associated to the pandemic there is a need for resurrecting the Families First Coronavirus Response Act that expired in 2020 to ensure pandemic related paid leave .

Higher education should also encourage the advancement of social policy from an Afrocentric perspective by creating and reforming policy to include the needs, beliefs, and perspectives of nontraditional graduate students of color in an effort to reduce the stressors associated with student work-life management. In this undertaking, it is important to understand that policy is an interdependent process that involves variations of nontraditional students. Policy then becomes an "expression of critical values, particularly for the individuals who develop, promote, and implement them (Bent-Goodley, Fairfax, & Carlton-LaNey, 2017, p. 4)."

Finally, relevant to research, qualitative and quantitative research is needed in the areas of student work-life balance and student work-life management for urban graduate students of color in various stages in matriculation, relationship status, and family composition. Additional research could focus on the multiple roles of urban matriculating parents and how they may or may not aid in student work-life management. Other research could explore how fellowship programs and mentorship for urban graduate students of color affect student work-life management. Finally, research is needed on the importance of accountability circles at predominantly white institutions for women of color.

A community culture underscores the importance of a collective concept of human identity, need, and shared experience; the more substantive and enduring reality of the unseen; and the interconnectedness of all people (Sealy, 2021). Although the insights gained are not generalizable, the importance of community to thrive in, connect, with decreasing stress and manage challenges associated with student-work-life management has been noted by the graduate students of this inquiry experience and is supported by the literature. The steady increase in graduate students of color who are categorized as nontraditional places pressure on institutions to provide a broader view of the academic community and include an array of support services. As a result, it becomes imperative to recognize that the one-size-fits-all educational model informing institutional cultures today is no longer valid (Polson, 2003).

REFERENCES

Alleman, A.-S., Allen Milton, S., Darrell, L., & Ofahengaue Vakalahi, H. F. (2018). Women of color and work-life balance in an urban environment: What is reality? *Urban Social Work, 2*(1), 80–95. https://doi.org/10.1891/2474-8684.2.1.80

Ani, M. (1994). *Let the circle be unbroken.* Ewing Township.

Asante, M. K. (2003). *Afrocentricity: The theory of social change.* Africa World Press.

Bent-Goodley, T. B. (2003). Policy implications of the criminal justice system for African American families and communities. In C. Munson & T. Bent-Goodley (Eds.), *African American social workers and social policy* (pp. 137-161). Routledge.

Bent-Goodley, T. B. (2005). An African centered approach to domestic violence. *Families in Society, 86*(2), 197–206. https://doi.org/10.1606/1044-3894.2455

Bent-Goodley, T., Fairfax, C. N., & Carlton-LaNey, I. (2017). The significance of African-centered social work for social work practice. *Journal of Human Behavior in the Social Environment, 27*(1-2), 1-6.

Bridges, D., & McGee, S. (2011). Collaborative inquiry: Reciprocity and authenticity. In Higgs, J., Titchen, A., Horsfall, D., Bridges, D. (Eds.), *Creative spaces for qualitative researching* (pp. 211-222). Brill Sense.

Boyd-Franklin, N. (1989). *Black families in therapy: A multisystems approach.* Guilford.

Braun, V., & Clarke, V. (2006). Using thematic analysis in psychology. *Qualitative Research in Psychology, 3*(2), 77-101.

Bray, J., Lee, J., Smith, L., & Yorks, L. (2000). *Collaborative inquiry in practice: Action, reflection, and meaning making.* Sage.

Brooks, A., & Watkins, K. E. (1994). A new era for action technologies: A look at the issues. *New Directions for Adult and Continuing Education, 1994*, 5–16. https://doi.org/10.1002/ace.36719946303

Brus, C. P. (2006). Seeking balance in graduate school: A realistic expectation or a dangerous dilemma? *New Directions for Student Services, 115*, 31–45. https://doi.org/10.1002/ss.214

Butler, A. B. (2007). Job characteristics and college performance and attitudes: A model of work-school conflict and facilitation. *The Journal of Applied Psychology, 92*(2), 500–510. https://doi.org/10.1037/0021-9010.92.2.500

Butler, J. P. (1992). Of kindred minds: The ties that bind. In M. A. Orlandi, R. Weston, & L. G. Epstein (Eds.), *Cultural competence for evaluators: A guide for alcohol and other drug abuse prevention practitioners working with ethnic/racial communities* (pp. 23–54). U.S. Department of Health & Human Services.

Campbell, F., & Valera, P. (2020). "The only thing new is the cameras": A study of US college students' perceptions of police violence on social media. *Journal of Black Studies, 51*(7), 654–670. https://doi.org/10.1177/0021934720935600

Chirikov, I., Soria, K. M., Horgos, B., & Jones-White, D. (2020). *Undergraduate and graduate students' mental health during the COVID-19 pandemic*. UC Berkeley Center for Studies in Higher Education. https://escholarship.org/uc/item/80k5d5hw

Choy, S. P. (2002). *Access & persistence: Findings from 10 years of longitudinal research on students* [ERIC Digest]. ERIC Clearinghouse on Higher Education. https://www.govinfo.gov/content/pkg/ERIC-ED466105/pdf/ERIC-ED466105.pdf

Darrell, L., Littlefield, M., & Washington, E. M. (2016). Safe spaces, nurturing places. *Journal of Social Work Education, 52*(1), 43-49.

Davies, A. R., & Frink, B. D. (2014). The origins of the ideal worker: The separation of work and home in the United States from the market revolution to 1950. *Work and Occupations, 41*(1), 18–39. https://doi.org/10.1177/0730888413515893

Davis, J. (2012). *School enrollment and work status: 2011*. U.S. Census Bureau. https://www.census.gov/library/publications/2012/acs/acsbr11-14.html

Dawson, M. C. (1994). *Behind the mule: Race and class in African American politics*. Princeton University Press.

Dolson, J. M., & Deemer, E. D. (2020). The relationship between perceived discrimination and school/work–family conflict among graduate student-parents. *Journal of Career Development* [Online first]. https://doi.org/10.1177/0894845320916245

Donohoo, J. (2013). *Collaborative inquiry for educators: A facilitator's guide to school improvement*. Corwin Press.

El-Ghoroury, N. H., Galper, D. I., Sawaqdeh, A., & Bufka, L. F. (2012). Stress, coping, and barriers to wellness among psychology graduate students. *Training and Education in Professional Psychology, 6*(2), 122–134. https://doi.org/10.1037/a0028768

Evans, T. M., Bira, L., Gastelum, J. B., Weiss, L. T., & Vanderford, N. L. (2018). Evidence for a mental health crisis in graduate education. *Nature Biotechnology, 36*(3), 282–284. https://doi.org/10.1038/nbt.4089

Fortuna, L. R., Tolou-Shams, M., Robles-Ramamurthy, B., & Porche, M. V. (2020). Inequity and the disproportionate impact of COVID-19 on communities of color in the United States: The need for a trauma-informed social justice response. *Psychological Trauma: Theory, Research, Practice, and Policy, 12*(5), 443–445. https://doi.org/10.1037/tra0000889

Fox, M., Snyder, T. D., & Connolly, B. A. (2005). *Youth indicators, 2005: Trends in the well-being of American youth* [NCES 2005-050]. National Center for

Gay, C., & Tate, K. (1998). Doubly bound: The impact of gender and race on the politics of
black women. *Political Psychology, 19*(1), 169-184.

Greenhaus, J. H., & Allen, T. D. (2011). Work-family balance: A review and extension of the literature. In J. C. Quick & L. E. Tetrick (Eds.), *Handbook of occupational health psychology* (pp. 165–183). American Psychological Association.

Holley, K. A., & Gardner, S. (2012). Navigating the pipeline: How socio-cultural influences impact first-generation doctoral students. *Journal of Diversity in Higher Education, 5*(2), 112–121. https://doi.org/10.1037/a0026840

Jaynes, G., & Williams, R. (1989). *A common destiny: Blacks and American society*. National Academy Press.

Kasl & Yorks, (2010). "Whose inquiry is this anyway?" Money, power, reports, and collaborative inquiry. *Adult Education Quarterly, 60*(4), 315-338.

King, A., & Herb, K. (2012). Putting the 'life' back into work-life balance for graduate students. *The Industrial-Organizational Psychologist, 49*(4), 125–129.

Lin, X. (2016). Barriers and challenges of female adult students enrolled in higher education: A literature review. *Higher Education Studies, 6*(2), 119–126. https://doi.org/10.5539/hes.v6n2p119

Martin, E. P., & Martin, J. M. (2002). *Spirituality and the Black helping tradition in social work*. NASW Press.

McCutcheon, J. M., & Morrison, M. A. (2018). It's "like walking on broken glass": Pan-Canadian reflections on work-family conflict from psychology women faculty and graduate students. *Feminism & Psychology, 28*(2), 231–252. https://doi.org/10.1177/0959353517739641

McPhatter, A. (2016). Urban social work with African Americans: Critical perspectives,
concepts, and theories. In R. Wells-Wilborn, A. McPhatter, & H. O. Vakalahi (Eds.), Social work practice with African Americans in urban environments (pp. 1–20). New York, NY: Springer.

National Center for Education Statistics. (n.d.). Nontraditional student definition. Retrieved July 16, 2021, from https://nces.ed.gov/pubs/web/97578e.asp

National Urban League. (2020). *State of Black America: Unmasked*. https://nul.org/state-of-black-america

Nodine, P. M., Arbet, J., Jenkins, P. A., Rosenthal, L., Carrington, S., Purcell, S. K., Lee, S., & Hoon, S. (2021). Graduate nursing student stressors during the COVID-19 pandemic. *Journal of Professional Nursing, 37*(4), 721–728. https://doi.org/10.1016/j.profnurs.2021.04.008

Okahana, H., Zhou, E., & Gao, J. (2020). Graduate enrollment and degrees: 2009-2019. Council of Graduate Schools.

Polson, C. J. (2003). Adult graduate students challenge institutions to change. *New Directions for Student Services, 102*, 59–68. https://doi.org/10.1002/ss.90

Riessman, C. K. (2008). *Narrative methods for the human sciences*. Sage.

Saldaña, J. (2014). Coding and analysis strategies. In Leavy, P. (Ed.), *The Oxford handbook of qualitative research*. Oxford University Press.

Schiele, J. H. (1996). Afrocentricity: An emerging paradigm in social work practice. *Social Work, 41*, 284–294.

Sealy, J. (2021). *Afrocentric perspective in social work*. YouTube. https://www.youtube.com/watch?v=OMX25KMlNKk

Seidman (2006). *Interviewing as qualitative research: A guide for researchers in education and the social sciences*. Teachers College Press.

Simien, E. M. (2005). Race, gender, and linked fate. *Journal of Black Studies, 35*(5), 529–550. https://doi.org/10.1177/0021934704265899

Springer, K. W., Parker, B. K., & Leviten-Reid, C. (2009). Making space for graduate student parents: Practice and politics. *Journal of Family Issues, 30*(4), 435-457.

Taylor, S. E. (2010). Social support: A review. In H. S. Friedman (Ed.), *Oxford handbook of health psychology*. Oxford University Press.

Theisen, M. R., McGeorge, C. R., & Walsdorf, A. A. (2018). Graduate student parents' perceptions of resources to support degree completion: Implications for family therapy programs. *Journal of Feminist Family Therapy, 30*(1), 46-70.

Walsh, B. A., Woodliff, T. A., Lucero, J., Harvey, S., Burnham, M. M., Bowser, T. L., Aguirre, M., & Zeh, D. W. (2021). Historically underrepresented graduate students' experiences during the COVID-19 pandemic. *Family Relations, 70*(4), 955–972. https://doi.org/10.1111/fare.12574

Wan Mohd Yunus, W., Badri, S., Panatik, S. A., & Mukhtar, F. (2021). The unprecedented movement control order (lockdown) and factors associated with the negative emotional symptoms, happiness, and work-life balance of Malaysian university students during the coronavirus disease (COVID-19) pandemic. *Frontiers in Psychiatry, 11*, 566221. https://doi.org/10.3389/fpsyt.2020.566221

Wilks, S. E. (2008). Resilience amid academic stress: The moderating impact of social support among social work students. *Advances in Social Work, 9*(2), 106–125. https://doi.org/10.18060/51

Wyland, R. L., Lester, S. W., Mone, M. A., & Winkel, D. E. (2013). Work and school at the same time? A conflict perspective of the work-school interface. *Journal of Leadership & Organizational Studies, 20*(3), 346–357.

SHARLENE ALLEN-MILTON, EdD, is an Assistant Professor in the School of Social Work with research interests in health and well-being, specifically work-life management for professional women and students of color as well as remote social work. Email: Sharlene.allen@morgan.edu.

NIA CALDWELLl, MSW, is a Licensed Master Level Social Worker that is a passionate advocate for mental health and community empowerment. Email: Niacaldwell@gmail.com.

DEVAL POPAT, M.S., is an Adjunct Professor in the School of Computer, Mathematical & Natural Sciences, and a Master's level student in the School of Social Work at Morgan State University. Email: Deval.popat@morgan.edu

TAVRIL PROUT, BSW, is a Master's level student in the School of Social Work at Morgan State University. Email: tapro2@morgan.edu.

CHERESE GODWIN, Ph.D. is an Assistant Professor in the School of Social Work at Temple University with research interests in social entrepreneurship and social policy. Email: Drcngodwin@gmail.com.

Manuscript submitted: ***July 08, 2021***
Manuscript revised: ***February 13, 2022***
Accepted for publication: ***February 17, 2022***

Peer-Reviewed Article

© *Journal of Underrepresented and Minority Progress*
Volume 6, Issue 1 (2022), pp. 97-120
ISSN: 2574-3465 Print/ ISSN: 2574-3481 Online
http://ojed.org/jump

Limbu Poets' Experiences of Using Facebook for Promoting Endangered Indigenous Language

Dig Dhoj Lawati
Karna Rana
Nepal Open University, Nepal

ABSTRACT

The authors report an examination of Limbu poets' experiences of using Facebook to share Limbu poems expecting to promote their Indigenous language, literature, and culture, and preserve Indigenous identities. We employed online semi-structured interviews with participants and observation of their Facebook walls to gather qualitative data. We discuss how the Limbu poets attempted to promote their Limbu language through Facebook. Limbu poets used their Indigenous poems to inform and promote the value of their language and to preserve Indigenous cultural values. The poetic creation in the Limbu language received significant responses from readers, however, far less than the poems in Nepali and English. This result may have occurred because many members of the Limbu community might not have understood Limbu poems. It demonstrates the decline of Limbu, one of the Indigenous languages in Nepal, and the challenge of preserving and promoting the language. Limbu poets' more organized and innovative ways of using Facebook for promoting their Indigenous language may help them achieve their aim to restore their language.

Keywords: Facebook, Limbu poets, Indigenous language, Marginalized community, Nepal

INTRODUCTION

Facebook, which was initially used to connect students at Harvard University, has become a global social networking website (Capua, 2012). The platform hosts nearly three billion users who exchange ideas and communicate with each other (Hutchinson, 2020). Facebook has become a common media source to share feelings and events publicly, teach students from home and discuss issues with members in closed groups (Giri & Rana, 2022). Teachers, writers, and researchers communicate their rhetorical writings, poems, and expressions about socio-cultural values and academic discourse through social media (DePew, 2011). Many people use Facebook for personal and mass communication, and educational activities (Aydin, 2012). Social media platforms such as Facebook, Twitter, and LinkedIn strengthen the scholarship of teachers, researchers, and students by increasing their academic communications (Sauter, 2014). Social media including Facebook can be a tool to strengthen relationships, ease communication and get entertainment (Kosinski et al., 2015; Rana, 2022). Facebook has become a medium to develop relationships with people, advertise businesses, and teach students.

Every medium of communication helps create an imaginative relationship between authors and their audiences (Brake, 2012). Writers can share their academic activities on personal blogs to attain self-directed satisfaction and communicate ideas through various pieces of writing such as poetic verses and lyrics with imagined audiences. Facebook and other social media platforms can help writers publish their literary arts and increase their popularity. However, Hanusch and Tandoc (2019) argue that responses from readers to writers' content on social media determine their level of engagement on social media and increase their number of followers. Diverse responses from readers on social media generate a distinct digital cultural heritage (Bareket-Bojmel et al., 2016). The growing use of Facebook has attracted researchers to study emerging cultures through the use of social networking sites. In recent years, it has become a medium for sharing Indigenous culture, language, and arts in Nepal. However, Phyak (2015) argues that Facebook language policing (i.e., homogeneity of language) in Nepal does not provide diverse space for linguistic heterogeneity and flexibility but creates monolingual ideologies which enforce hegemony. The iconization of Nepali as a national language and English as a language of technology and universal market narrows the language space for minoritized people to use their native languages on Facebook and in other spaces (Phyak, 2015). Sharma (2012), for example, reports that college students create their bilingual identity by blending local and English languages on Facebook. Although rare, Indigenous languages are present on Facebook walls, as Facebook has somewhat become a space for Indigenous languages in recent years. However, Limbu, one of the 129 Indigenous languages in Nepal (Khabarhub, 2022), is rarely seen on Facebook walls. Although the Limbu language has its script, dictionary, and grammar, the systematic exclusion of Indigenous languages including Limbu from education and official functions for centuries (Phyak, 2015) jeopardized its presence on social media as one such consequence.

This paper examines Limbu poets' use of Facebook to promote their Indigenous language through poetic creations. The analysis of Limbu poets' experiences of using Facebook to share Limbu poems and the discourses obtained from Facebook walls of both poets and other participants is reported in this paper. This study is noteworthy because it opens a new way of conducting social media research by exploring Facebook discourses about an ethnic language. We also attempt to examine how the social media interaction between Limbu poets and their readers contributes to building a distinct digital ethnic culture.

Creative Discourse on Social Media

Social networking websites have become common tools to develop communities of learning and where people share ideas publicly (Kuss & Griffiths, 2017). For example, studies in Saudi Arabia (Al-Jarf, 2015, 2018) reported that Arabian Facebook users shared poems, short stories, feelings, personal experiences, and proverbs written in literary style. Wu and colleagues (2016) found that social media produced social, informative and habitual capital which increased users' creative performance on social network sites in Taiwan. In their study in Taiwan, Chai and Fan (2017) reported that the use of social media helped the students of design education increase their creativity. Moreover, Rahmah (2018) found that Quick, a video editing app, and Instagram provided students with a digital platform for creative writing to enhance their learning experiences and writing in English in Indonesia. Similarly, Ali and colleagues (2019) revealed that teamwork on social media increased the efficiency of a team's creative knowledge and performance in China. Creativity and innovation on social media rely on technology (Ratten, 2017). Some studies (Flew, 2018; Miller, 2016) demonstrate that social media provides enthusiasts with unique and innovative opportunities for extending their social connection and sharing creative art and product.

How social media operators use these platforms to publish their art increases the value of social media for communicating ideas (Miller, 2016). For example, Li and Duan (2018) found that the blog, Weibo, played an important role in promoting cultural sites and museums in China. Marchukov (2016) discussed how the use of websites and social media strengthened the cultural diplomacy of Germany and Japan. Especially, both the countries chose their official websites and social media platforms to share and promote their cultures and arts and it helped to promote their national culture abroad. Kavakci and Kraeplin's (2016) study demonstrated that Muslim women living in European countries constructed online identities by using Facebook, Twitter, and YouTube as tools to advertise fashionable hijab (a religious scarf to cover a woman's head and hair). The authors argued that, although the publicly visible women's presentation of hijabs would not represent all those typically used hijabs across all Muslim communities, the technological advancement changed religious beliefs, traditions, and values. The growing use of social media for personal, professional, and social communications has also transferred and made socio-cultural properties visible across the world (Meikle, 2016).

Indigenous Languages on Social Media

Some researchers have focused on social media posts to analyze the presence of Indigenous languages (Outakoski et al., 2018; Rice et al., 2016). For example, we know that the presence of Maori, a minority language of New Zealand, on social media increasingly promoted the development and preservation of the language (Keegan et al., 2015; Waitoa et al., 2015). Lindgren and Cocq (2017) reported that Twitter enabled marginalized communities to communicate with other similar groups and share their common interest on a global scale. However, Wyburn (2018) found that the dominant use of English on social media imperilled the Welsh language in Ireland. Some studies reported that hashtag tweets in Welsh, Irish, and Frisian languages significantly increased the use of these languages (Ferré-Pavia et al., 2018; McMonagle et al., 2019). Similar studies (Jongbloed-Faber et al., 2016; Jongbloed-Faber et al., 2017) in the Netherlands identified that the use of Frisian and Dutch languages on Twitter rapidly attracted the speakers of these languages and increased the number of followers.

Social media has become a powerful tool to promote Indigenous languages in many countries. For example, Facebook became instrumental in the process of revitalising Maya, an Indigenous language in Mexico (Cru, 2015). In particular, the use of Spanish and Maya together on Facebook functioned as a language lesson for youths. The strategy of making Maya visible on Facebook, a bottom-up approach, significantly increased the number of Maya users and the chance of increasing legitimacy from the government. Similarly, Stern (2017) found that Facebook groups are an effective tool to encourage the use of Balinese in Indonesia. Especially, her strategy of following those who did not want to join Balinese Facebook group increased the number of members particularly teens in the group and the likelihood that they would continue to use Balinese as their main language. Deschene (2019) reported that the use of social media and websites to share audio-visual materials of Coptic, an endangered Egyptian language, attracted a significant number of viewers and most viewers expressed an interest in learning the language. Other studies found that the use of social media for the revival of Indigenous languages such as Maori in New Zealand (Lee, 2018), Udmurt in Russia (Pischlöger, 2016) and Low German in northern Germany (Wiggers, 2017) significantly promoted the use of these languages in common communications in the respective countries. For the promotion of Indigenous languages, Belmar and Glass (2019) suggest Indigenous people consistently boost their virtual communication on social media. These studies indicate how social media help promote and preserve Indigenous languages. Unfortunately, there is limited literature particularly focused on the use of Indigenous language in poetic arts on social media.

Narrative, Identity Construction, and Blogging Status on Social Media

Some scholars have focused their study on identity construction, story posts, and blogging updates on social media. For example, Dayter (2015) and Page (2010) revealed that short narrative stories on social media were not literary work, but they were sources to understand the concepts of narrative theory. Jeon and Mauney (2014) reported that political face work on social media was intended to negotiate and discuss the online identity of communicators and to keep the face stable by bringing a new strategy. Gündüz (2017) argues that status updates on social media are mainly related to identity construction, positioning oneself among friends and building cultural identities. Alsaggaf (2015), for example, reported that Saudi women's use of the Arabian language on social media to share their socio-cultural activities helped them establish their identity. Shlezak (2015) investigated that narrative writing on Facebook helped adults construct new social identities. Gonzalez-Polledo and Tarr (2016) reported a significant contribution of Flickr and Tumblr apps to develop communities of common language users.

Micro-blogging and status updates on social media which belong to local languages and literacy practices are usually not included in the curricular activities of educational institutions and the government (Zhang & Ren, 2020). For example, Outakoski and colleagues (2018) reported that, although Sapmi, an Indigenous language in northern Europe, was systematically used on Twitter, blogs, YouTube videos, and personalized mobile apps to attract native speakers, it did not get a significant number of readers. Sharma and Phyak (2017) argue that the exclusion of Indigenous languages from education and official functions, and the imposition of the English language in education in Nepal have jeopardized Indigenous languages. However, McDaniel and colleagues (2012) earlier suggested that the use of one's mother tongue on social media to share ideas and creations would help develop a bond among the speakers of the languages and preserve minority languages. In particular, social media can be an instructional tool for learners of Indigenous languages (Carpenter & Krutka, 2015). For example, Guta and Karolak (2015) reported that Saudi Arabian women's blogging in the Arabian language enabled them to build a strong community of their language and fight against the hegemony of foreign languages. Liu and colleagues (2016) emphasize that the use of minority languages on web blogs can motivate their speakers to explore local values, cultures, and identities. Li and colleagues (2018) argue that web blogs can be instrumental to preserve the diversity of language, culture, and traditions.

Current Study

In absence of local literature, international studies provide a picture of how the use of various social media platforms helped promote the use of Indigenous languages. In particular, the use of Facebook to share Arabic poems, stories, and personal experiences in Saudi Arabia (Al-Jarf, 2018), other social media platforms to preserve Maori in New Zealand (Keegan et al., 2015; Waitoa et al., 2015), and the use of Twitter to promote the Frisian and Dutch languages (Jongbloed-Faber et al., 2016; Jongbloed-Faber et al., 2017) significantly increased the use of those Indigenous languages. Moreover, the practice of Facebook to revitalize an Indigenous language in Mexico (Cru, 2015) and encourage the use of Balinese in Indonesia (Stern, 2017) are related to the purpose of the current study: to examine how Facebook would help Limbu poets to preserve Limbu language, culture, and literature. The following research questions were posed: (1) What are Limbu poets' experiences of using Facebook to share Limbu poems? (2) What is the perception of Limbu speakers towards Limbu poets' use of Facebook to share Limbu poems? and (3) What is Limbu speakers' motivation towards their mother tongue?

METHODS

Participants

The participants in this study were Limbu Indigenous people who spoke Limbu as their mother tongue and Nepali as a link language (i.e., a language to communicate with other language speakers). Participants also used Facebook to share Limbu poems or comment on other poems on Facebook. Their age ranged from 25 to 50. Some participants from Nepal lived in the Eastern Hills of the country or lived in cities after migrating from the Eastern Hills. Participants from Sikkim (a state of India bordered by Nepal) resided in villages and cities.

We selected participants based on their use of Facebook to post and comment on Limbu poetry. In particular, we focused on those who used Facebook at least once a week to post or comment on poems. Participants were four Limbu poets and four readers. Most participants were from Nepal, while three Limbu poets were from Sikkim. Table 1 summarizes the participants' demographics. Participants' names are replaced by pseudonyms to maintain anonymity.

Table 1
Participant Location and Demographic Information

Participant	Location	Sex	Age
Sese (Poet)	Panchthar District (Middle East Nepal: Hills)	Male	31
Parajungung (Poet)	Panchthar District (Middle East Nepal: Hills)	Male	40
Seri (Poet)	Panchthar District (Middle East Nepal: Hills)	Male	28
Khohang (Poet)	Jhapa District (South-East Nepal: Terai)	Male	45

Parajung (Reader)	Panchthar District (Middle East Nepal: Hills)	Male	35
Larang (Reader)	Tehrathum District (Middle East Nepal: Hills)	Male	36
Niyara (Reader)	Ilam District (Middle East Nepal: Hills)	Male	34
Semi (Reader)	Dhankuta District (Middle East Nepal: Hills)	Male	36
Pahang (Poet)	Sikkim (North-East State, India)	Male	48
Mukla (Poet)	Sikkim (North-East State, India)	Male	44
Sesephung (Poet)	Sikkim (North-East State, India)	Male	36

Research Instrument

An interview protocol was used to conduct interviews with the participants. A list of questions guided the interviews and issues raised by participants during the interviews were used to continue the conversation. The questions posed to participants are listed in Table 2.

Table 2
Interview Questions

Lead questions to poets are as follows:
a. How is your experience of using Facebook to share Limbu poems?
b. In what ways do you promote the use of the Limbu language?
c. Why do you choose Facebook to share Limbu poems?
e. What is your expectation of writing Limbu poems and sharing them on Facebook?
f. If you expect to preserve the Limbu language, culture and literature through poems, how does it work?
g. Which script do you often use to write and share poems?
h. If you prefer to use the Limbu script, why?
Lead questions to readers of Limbu poems are as follows:
a. How is your perception of sharing Limbu poems on Facebook?
b. What do you think about the contribution of Limbu poems in the preservation of Limbu language, culture and literature?
c. In what ways do you respond to Limbu poets?
d. How is your perception of using Facebook to share Limbu poems?
e. If you expect to preserve the Limbu language, culture and literature through poems, how does it work?
f. Which script do you often use to comment on poems?
g. If you prefer to use the Limbu script, why?

Although a specific rating scale or a checklist was not used to observe the poets and readers' activities on Facebook walls, our observation was guided by the language they used, the content they discussed, and prompt comments and replies. In addition, the issues raised in the interviews also led to our observation of participants' Facebook walls.

Procedure

After we obtained ethics approval from our institution, we recruited participants by identifying potential participants through Facebook. We obtained informed consent by emailing both information sheet and consent form through email. We asked participants to accept our friend request on their Facebook accounts, which allowed us to view their Facebook walls and communicate through messenger. We then sent a request through Facebook Messenger to about 15 Limbu poets and 15 readers of Limbu poems on Facebook asking for their participation with the hope that we would recruit eight poets and four readers of Limbu poems. Only seven poets expressed interest in participating in this study and four readers participated.

We used qualitative research methods to examine Limbu poets' experiences using Facebook to share Limbu poems with Limbu speakers. We employed online semi-structured interviews and observation which allowed us to gather Limbu poets and their poem readers' experiences of using Facebook to share Limbu poems and comment on them. Online semi-structured interviews were conducted with the participants on multiple occasions by using a mobile phone and Facebook Messenger. The voice feature of Facebook Messenger was used to interview participants as the video was not used. All the interviews were recorded on a mobile phone. The interview protocol was administered in Limbu.

Conducting an observation of participants' Facebook posts and comments strengthened the interview data. Participants' Facebook walls were followed for about three months. The first author visited participants' Facebook walls daily to note Limbu poets' shared content and to see readers' comments on poets' poems. Poets and Limbu poetry readers' comments on Facebook were recorded on a smartphone and also stored on a laptop. Specifically, screenshots of their public communications on their personal Facebook were stored on these devices.

Data Analysis

We analyzed interview and observation data following the principles of thematic analysis. First, the first author, who speaks Limbu, transcribed interview audio records and translated them into the English language. Then, we generated themes and organized the data into those themes. In particular, an inductive coding scheme (Braun & Clarke, 2006) helped identify themes, organize the data gathered through interviews and observations, and analyze the data. We read various archived documents such as journal articles, books, reports, theses, and websites against the data gathered through interviews and observations.

FINDINGS

This section demonstrates the data analysis of interviews and observations by its outstanding themes.

Limbu speakers' perception of using Facebook to promote Limbu language

Observations of Limbu poets' Facebook posts and their poetry readers' responses, and interviews with them showed that most participants significantly used Facebook for approaching readers. Because it is the most popular social networking site in Nepal (Giri & Rana, 2022), they preferred Facebook to other social media platforms. Participants identified it as highly accessible for readers, as responses from the virtual world are not possible in the traditional way of publishing and printing books. For example, Sese, a poet, said:

> There is an increasing number of readers of creations in the Limbu language on Facebook. Our collective creations on Facebook have created some literary trends worldwide. I am very satisfied with the responses of the audience. I hope I will get more Limbu readers.

Sese's comment indicated that there are some Limbu speakers, who followed Limbu language poets. The poems that appeared on Facebook created literary trends and movement because Limbu speakers had a sense of affection and pride in their mother tongue. They found that the audience liked their poems, which motivated them to create poetry and post them on social media. However, few participants among the poets were practicing writing and post poems in more than one language. For example:

> They read and liked my poems. Some hit likes by reading and others without reading. I have got friends from different language communities like Nepali, Magar and Rai. When I post Nepali poems, I get likes and comments from Nepali language users. (Pahang, poet)

Pahang's expression reflected that Limbu poets kept the audience in their minds while posting their poems on social media. They posted short poems in Limbu and Nepali languages to reach both language speakers. Their strategy of using both languages provides a picture of how Limbu poets tried to develop their popularity and gain higher social respect from wider communities. Poets remained active in posting their poems on Facebook because they believed the readers were engaged in the poems they shared. Parajungung, a poet, said:

> There are many readers of Limbu poems posted on Facebook. Facebook seems a friendly place for those poets who are from Indigenous communities. Nowadays, when they post their poems, they immediately get responses. So, they prefer to use social media to reach readers.

His expression reflected that he, an Indigenous poet, intended to promote the value of the Limbu language through the development of poetry and increase the awareness of the language in the community. The increasing reactions to the Limbu poems on Facebook indicated the growth of people's awareness of the Limbu language as well as the creation of poetry. For example, Larang, a reader of Limbu poems on Facebook, said:

> I have responded to the poems on Facebook. I often hit like and comments but sometimes I don't get a response from poets. I comment in Limbu and many others also use Limbu. This is how we can promote the use of Limbu in conversations.

His comments provided a much clearer picture of how Limbu poets' Facebook approach contributed to increasing the use of the Limbu language in the discourses on Facebook. His idea would have motivated many other Limbu speakers to use their mother tongue in common communication too.

Mother Language Motivation

We explored Limbu poets' expectation to restore Limbu, one of the endangered Indigenous languages in Nepal, and develop Limbu literature and culture. Poets appreciated that Facebook was an appropriate and friendly tool for sharing creative writings in the mother language. They were aware that on social media they could rapidly spread their poems and get immediate responses from readers. Their strategy of using two languages (Nepali and Limbu) increased their social connection within Nepal and across the world with people who could read their poems. Parajung, a reader of Limbu poem, said:

> Nowadays Limbu poets even can use Sirijunga script on webs and social media because it is already registered in Unicode. I find even the poems and comments in Sirijunga script. Facebook is one of the best tools to make Limbu people aware of their language.

Parajung's observation about the Limbu poets' space on Facebook indicates that they were well-informed about social media and its capacity to connect with many people. His comment provided a clear picture of how the Limbu poem was expected to increase the value of the Limbu language and promote its use. Facebook would have helped them reach the unreached Limbu community and speakers across the world. They expected that social media including Facebook would help them develop their mother language, literature, and culture.

Poets' expectations of promoting the Indigenous language reflected how they could preserve their Indigenous identities. They, thus, seemed to choose Facebook to share Limbu poems as an instrument to make Limbu people aware of their language, literature, and culture. Facebook was found to support the Limbu language and its script. The Limbu poets and their readers were able to interact in their script on Facebook. The responses they received from readers motivated them to use Facebook to promote their language through poetry.

> Only few posts appear in the mother tongue. More writings appear in English and Nepali on my wall. Though Limbu people are settled all around the world, only few people are there who can read and write in their mother tongue. (Mukla, poet)

Mukla's comment indicates how Limbu language speakers are decreasing and the language is declining from communities. It indicates that it is essential for Limbu speakers to seek the inclusion of their Indigenous language in education to save it. Poets' initiative of publishing poems in their language has, at some level, developed an awareness of their Limbu language, culture, and literature. They could use their own Sirijunga script of the Limbu language on Facebook to let people know about the unique script. It was observed on their Facebook walls that few poets and readers could read and interact in their mother tongue. However, the majority of readers who engaged in interaction used Nepali and English scripts. Limited comments in Sirijunga script on poems indicated that there were few, who could understand the Limbu language and were aware of Limbu poems. In comparison to the writers of Nepali poems, the Limbu poems occupied little space on Facebook. Seri, a poet, said:

> There is no value of Limbu poems as Nepali literature gains, though we sometimes post better Limbu poems than Nepali poems. I do not find a friendly environment on Facebook for Indigenous poets like me. When I post Nepali poems, they get more likes and comments than my Limbu poems.

It was a difficult job for Limbu poets to promote their Indigenous language in a context where only Nepali is the language of Education and administration. Her frustration reflects the grounded reality because most people understand the Nepali language. The speakers of the Limbu language are fewer, and it gets a limited number of readers. Limbu poets would have realized that the number of speakers determines the promotion of specific literature in a particular language. Although they consistently published poems in the Limbu language and sometimes in Nepali, their publication of poems in Nepali received far more responses than the poems in their Limbu language. This tendency significantly increased poets' frustration that Limbu, one of the Indigenous languages, may rapidly decline in the communities. It also indicated that Indigenous poets were underrated and ignored by many social media users. It might have happened because of the minority language. In both Nepal and Sikkim, the Nepali language is the language of communication, education, and office. The Nepali language is dominant over the Limbu language and Limbu poets received limited responses in their Indigenous language. Most readers, who were Limbu speakers, were not interested in creative writing in the mother language. Their expressions reflected that they would not care about what was shared in their language on Facebook. For example, Khohang said:

> I do not find there is a positive view for those writers, readers, and mother tongue on Facebook. Facebook users are only in provocative posts. They are not interested in language, literature, and culture. Only those close companions react positively but they do not go thoroughly in my posts. Most of the people from the same community remain indifferent. They even do not hit like, comment, and share.

Khonang's comment indicated that Limbu speakers have a low level of awareness of their language, literature, and culture. His comment showed the gradual decline of Limbu and similar Indigenous languages from communities. Limbu speakers' lack of interest in their Limbu language poems provides a much clearer picture of how it is losing social existence. For example, Semi, a reader of Limbu poem, said:

> There are Limbu poets who write in the Nepali language to become popular but they don't write in Limbu. Many Limbu people cannot read the script. There is a lack of awareness of the mother tongue in the Limbu community. Because of that, a lot of people can't read and write in their mother tongue. So, in my opinion, though the Facebook platform is suitable, Limbu people don't understand the importance of literature, culture, and tradition. There are not many readers for Limbu poems.

Other participants echoed that they saw Indigenous identity in crisis and the challenges of regaining it. Because the Indigenous languages have been excluded from education and administration for centuries, an individual effort such as the Limbu poets' initiative in this study might not be adequate to revitalize the Indigenous languages and restore Indigenous identities. However, the poets in this study had a high level of motivation to reach out to maximum Limbu speakers with poems through Facebook, increase their awareness of Indigenous identities, and restore them.

Facebook as a Means of Restoring Limbu Language, Culture, and Literature

It was evident from interviews and observations that the Limbu people expressed their frustration and stress against the decline of social and cultural identities. At the same time, they showed their will to revive their declining identities through Facebook. For example, Limbu poets' Facebook wall showed their proactive engagement with poetic content where they frequently posted their poems in their mother language and commented on others' posts. They appreciated the interactive features of Facebook such as sharing, commenting, and tagging that allowed them to reach out to a wide range of readers across the world and promote the practice of writing poems in their Limbu language. Their expressions reflected their motivation of gaining space in the formal education for their Indigenous language and getting justice. For example, Sese, a poet, shared:

> These Limbu folk poetic forms are not taught at any universities of the world but on Facebook, it is possible to study, share, and comment. Whatever I post on Facebook, I immediately get a reply which is not possible in the case of printed books. There is a tool to get a reply and interact with readers on Facebook. It is like a university.

He wished that the universities would have included the Limbu language in the curriculum and allowed people to learn about Limbu culture, values, and arts. Unfortunately, none of such languages is covered by the higher education curriculum. He, therefore, appreciated Facebook for being a source of sharing and learning Limbu poems. For example, Parajung, a reader of Limbu poems, said:

> In a traditional way of publishing and producing books and magazines, readers get those things after long, but social media made it easy to read on their devices. As soon as they post something on social media, they get responses from the audience. From those responses, Limbu poets get a chance to improve their creations.

Parajung's expression reflected how Facebook became instrumental to promote the use of the Limbu language and contribute to restoring its declining status. Because Facebook allowed Limbu poets to share their literature, particularly with the people from Limbu communities, the poets were, at some level, successful to attract many Limbu people to their poems, and increase the Limbu people's awareness of their Indigenous language, literature, and culture. Quick responses from readers helped Limbu poets improve their creations in their mother tongue and accelerate their initiative of reaching out to maximum readers across the world. None of the poets had the stress of the number of readers of their Limbu poems, although they were worried about how the speakers of the Limbu language are rapidly declining.

> I interact with them. Some readers guess the meaning of my poems and others comment that they do not understand my words. Some complain that I use myths unknown to them. Many people may not know typical Limbu terms and phrases. (Sesephung, poet)

Sesephung's comment provided a picture of why many readers did not understand the typical poetic language of Limbu. The exclusion of the Limbu language from education and administration was probably one of the major causes that prevented Limbu people to learn the typical Limbu language, especially the poetic genre. Readers who could generally speak the Limbu language were probably just literate but not highly educated. For example, Sese, a poet said:

> Discriminatory language policy has endangered many Indigenous languages including Limbu. For centuries, only Nepali [has been] used in administration and as a medium of instruction in education. Indigenous languages were excluded from education. Instead of promoting local languages, the government has allowed schools to use English as a medium of instruction. Although the recent constitution states the right to basic education in the mother tongue, it is yet to be implemented.

Future studies can further investigate how Limbu speakers' level of education plays a role in their understanding of Limbu poetic language. However, poets' comments indicated Limbu speakers' increasing engagement in the Limbu language. This suggests that Facebook became instrumental to increase Limbus' awareness of the Limbu language, culture, and literature.

> When I post Nepali poems, I get likes and comments from Nepali language users. Some readers respond to me by messaging on Facebook messenger. Some readers give me the advice to publish those poems in the anthology. Some readers respond by calling me. (Pahang, poet)

Pahang sounded that Facebook significantly contributed to the promotion of Limbu poems which implied the preservation of the Limbu language. Especially live communication features such as comments and chat allowed both poets and readers to share their experiences and ideas about poems and their mother language. Both poets and readers expected that the people of their community would have channelled their practice of sharing ideas on Facebook to educational activities to promote the use of the Limbu language in daily communication.

> As far as I see the likes and comments on Limbu poets' poems on Facebook, I think they are being inspired and praised to move ahead by the reader audience. Facebook readers seem to encourage them to create more and post more Limbu poems. I think Limbu poets get inspiration to keep on creating poems. My comments on their poems are taken positively by Limbu poets. (Niyara, Reader)

Niyara's comments provide a picture of how readers' responses energized Limbu poets to promote their Indigenous language through Facebook. In particular, their use of Facebook for sharing Limbu poems was found to be instrumental and that might have contributed to the Limbu community's initiative for restoring their Indigenous language, culture, and literature.

DISCUSSION

Findings suggest that Limbu poets' interest in publishing their Limbu poems on Facebook emerged from the motive of promoting the Limbu language. Limbu poets appreciated Facebook that it allowed them to share their poems and reach out to a large number of readers, which was not possible in the traditional way of publishing and printing books. Some poets reported that they intended to increase the number of readers by posting short poems which would be comfortable for readers to read. One of the readers observed that Limbu poets had an increasing readership and quick responses to their poems in the Limbu language on Facebook. Responses from readers enabled Limbu poets to improve their creations and increase the number of readers across the world. Limbu poets' initiative of using Facebook to share their poems in their Limbu language greatly contributed to the promotion of the Limbu language, literature, and cultural value. It was, to some extent, consistent with the findings of Bigelow and colleagues (2017) in the United States, a different context, that the use of social media in language classrooms enabled students to develop culturally and linguistically rich content for global audiences.

Mainstream education is based on either Nepali or English or both languages although students have the right to education in their mother tongue (Rana, 2018). Some studies (Phyak, 2013; Sah, 2020) suggest ensuring the implementation of mother-tongue-based education to promote the use of local languages and ease teaching and learning in students' mother tongues. However, the exclusion of Indigenous languages from education and administration (Rana & Sah, forthcoming) has alienated those languages from many Indigenous families and made it difficult to preserve them as Indigenous identities. Thus, Facebook can be a platform for identity construction (Ditchfield, 2020) and the development of Indigenous people's awareness of their language, literature, and culture.

Connecting many Limbu people scattered across the world, however, seemed to be a challenging job for Limbu poets. Also, many Limbu descendants might have lost their family language because of the Nepali language (Phyak, 2019). It was evident from interviews that the majority of Facebook users were more comfortable reading poems in Nepali and English than in Limbu. Moreover, poems in the Nepali language received more comments than poems in Limbu. It has happened because the population of Limbu language users is far less than Nepali speakers. In addition, many people could not read Sirijunga script although Limbu poets preferred to use their unique script on social media to promote their language. However, one of the readers observed that only a few poems in Sirijunga script appeared on his Facebook wall. Readers appreciated interaction in their Sirijunga script on Facebook. One of the poets, however, expressed his frustration that most of the elite Limbu people did not show any interest in his poems. Limited comments on Limbu script poems indicate the gradual decline of the Limbu language from the communities. Poets and readers' experiences indicated that Nepali and English, the dominant languages on social media, influenced Limbu, a marginalized Indigenous language. The discriminatory language policy that excluded Indigenous languages from education and administration (Sharma & Phyak, 2017) might have jeopardized the Limbu language. In this situation, Igboanusi and Peter (2004) suggest maximizing the use of Indigenous languages in common communication to revive the endangered languages.

It was evident from interviews and observations that the online communication feature of Facebook played a significant role to promote and preserve the Limbu language. Communicative features such as like, share, tag, and group on Facebook, however, enabled Limbu poets to interact with a large number of readers. Poets, thus, appreciated the interactive features on Facebook which enabled them to engage in communication with readers. Some readers observed that Limbu poets were motivated by immediate responses to their poems on Facebook. Poets received an increasing number of comments following their regular posts of Limbu poems on Facebook. It indicated how the number of readers of Limbu poetry on Facebook was increasing. It reminded the findings of Honeycutt and Cunliffe (2010) in Wales that Facebook significantly increased the use of Welsh which gradually came to be a language of common communication. Although the interactions in the Limbu language on Facebook indicated the increasing use of the language, it was not visible whether Limbu speakers increased the use of their Indigenous language in their daily communication.

Limbu poets, however, were aware of the capacity of social media to reach many people across the world. They were striving to promote their language and use it on social media. Limbu poets and their readers were found engaged in interaction in their language. They were introducing their identical script to their readers from the Limbu community. However, the use of the Limbu language was less than the Nepali and English languages on Facebook. This account of experiences indicated that the minority of Limbu speakers were compelled to use their mother tongue and another dominant language on social media. This finds a resonance in the findings of Shafie and Nayan (2013) in Malaysia, a different context, that, although the Bahasa language was used as a base language on Facebook walls, English words were frequently mixed in writings. It indicates a threat from dominant languages such as Nepali to many Indigenous languages including Limbu that are seeking cultural restoration in Nepal.

Limbu poets, therefore, expressed their frustration that they had limited Limbu speakers. Most users were indifferent toward creative writing in their mother language. Limbu poets had a belief that they were found underrated and ignored by many Facebook users. It indicated that Limbu poetry received a low level of readers' attention on Facebook. It, to some extent, resonates with the findings of Androutsopoulos (2015) who reported that readers always have the flexibility to choose their comfortable language to communicate on social media which determines the promotion of the diversity of cultural discourses. The findings of the present study suggest that many Facebook users, albeit they were from Limbu communities and could speak their Indigenous language, probably had a low level of awareness of their language value or were uninterested in their community language. Limbu poets expressed their frustration that they were unable to get a highly motivating environment on Facebook for writers and their creative writing in the Limbu language. Although findings showed the Limbu people's increasing awareness of their language, literature, and culture following the poets' poems and comments on them, the poets expressed their dissatisfaction with the level of Limbu speakers' awareness of their Indigenous identities. They perceived that the level of effort they applied to restore the Limbu language, literature, and culture through Facebook was inadequate. They probably needed to explore a much more innovative way of using Facebook not only for sharing poems and replying to readers' comments but also for increasing Limbu speakers' understanding of their social and cultural identities and participating in their initiative. It might help them achieve similar to the findings of Velázquez (2017) in Spain who found that Spanish people preferred to use Spanish on social media to promote their language and culture. The organized effort of using Facebook would help promote minority languages (Cunliffe, 2019). Limbu poets in this study had a low level of expectation that Facebook would help preserve their Indigenous language as an identity. It indicates the challenges of preserving the Limbu language and its creative poetic arts. However, the participants in this study had a motivation to explore more innovative ideas of utilizing Facebook to develop an organized effort to promote their Indigenous language, literature, and culture.

CONCLUSION

Limbu poets' use of Facebook for sharing poems in the Limbu language was expected to promote their Limbu language, literature, and cultural value. Their initiatives attracted readers from across the world and there was an increasing number of readers of their poems on Facebook. They received quick responses from readers, and it motivated them to share more poems on Facebook. However, although they had many Limbu speakers connected on Facebook, only a few people actively engaged in poems and commented on them. In this process, the online communication features of Facebook played a significant role for Limbu poets to shape their poetry and engage with readers. Communicative features of Facebook enabled Limbu poets to reach many readers across the world. The language feature of Facebook allowed them to introduce and create poems in their Sirijunga Limbu script and communicate with their readers on Facebook. However, the users of the Limbu language were compelled to use the Limbu language and another dominant language – Nepali or English – on Facebook. Unfortunately, Limbu, an Indigenous language, received far less response than the Nepali language from readers.

Because the Limbu language is excluded from education and administration for centuries, it has lost its formal status with the decline of its users. While Nepali and English are dominantly used on social media including Facebook, the Limbu language occupied very limited space on Facebook. However, Limbu poets consistently raised their voice through poems to promote their Indigenous language, literature, and culture. Nevertheless, they had frustration following the low-level participation of Limbu speakers in their poems on Facebook. Many Limbu speakers probably had a low level of awareness of their language which prevented them from extensively using their language in communication on Facebook. It indicated the gradual decline of Limbu speakers and their language. In particular, the Limbu language, one of the endangered languages in Nepal, may die if it is not timely promoted in education or so. It suggests including Indigenous languages in education for restorative justice.

Finally, this study included a limited number of participants who were only identified as male, because we were unable to recruit female participants. Data from a more diverse sample of participants across more districts of Nepal and Sikkim may help generate much more powerful findings.

Acknowledgements
We wish to thank all the participants in the study and acknowledge that the study was conducted in the original lands of the Limbu people.

Declaration of conflicting interests
The author(s) declared no potential conflicts of interest with respect to the research, authorship, and/or publication of this article.

Funding
We have received no funding from any organization.

REFERENCES

Ali, A., Wang, H., & Khan, A. N. (2019). Mechanism to enhance team creative performance through social media: A transactive memory system approach. *Computers in Human Behavior, 91*, 115-126. https://doi.org/10.1016/j.chb.2018.09.033

Al-Jarf, R. (2015). Discourse and creativity issues in EFL creative writing on Facebook. *International Journal of Signs and Semiotic Systems (IJSSS), 4*(1), 54-81. https://doi.org/10.4018/978-1-5225-5622-0.ch001

Al-Jarf, R. (2018). Exploring discourse and creativity in Facebook creative writing by non-native speakers. In M. Danesi (Ed.), *Empirical research on semiotics and visual rhetoric* (pp. 1-31). IGI Global. https://doi.org/10.4018/978-1-5225-5622-0.ch001

Alsaggaf, R. M. (2015). *Identity construction and social capital: A qualitative study of the use of Facebook by Saudi women* [Doctoral thesis, University of Leicester]. England. https://leicester.figshare.com/account/articles/10160807

Androutsopoulos, J. (2015). Networked multilingualism: Some language practices on Facebook and their implications. *International Journal of Bilingualism, 19*(2), 185-205. https://doi.org/10.1177/1367006913489198

Aydin, S. (2012). A review of research on Facebook as an educational environment. *Educational Technology Research and Development, 60*(6), 1093-1106. https://doi.org/10.1007/s11423-012-9260-7

Bareket-Bojmel, L., Moran, S., & Shahar, G. (2016). Strategic self-presentation on Facebook: Personal motives and audience response to online behavior. *Computers in Human Behavior, 55*, 788-795. https://doi.org/10.1016/j.chb.2015.10.033

Belmar, G., & Glass, M. (2019). Virtual communities as breathing spaces for minority languages: Re-framing minority language use in social media. *Adeptus* (14). https://doi.org/10.11649/a.1968

Bigelow, M., Vanek, J., King, K., & Abdi, N. (2017). Literacy as social (media) practice: Refugee youth and native language literacy at school. *International Journal of Intercultural Relations, 60*, 183-197. https://doi.org/10.1016/j.ijintrel.2017.04.002

Brake, D. R. (2012). Who do they think they're talking to? Framings of the audience by social media users. *International Journal of Communication, 6*, 1056–1076. https://ijoc.org/index.php/ijoc/article/view/932/747

Braun, V., & Clarke, V. (2006). Using thematic analysis in psychology. *Qualitative Research in Psychology, 3*(2), 77-101. https://doi.org/10.1191/1478088706qp063oa

Capua, I. D. (2012). A literature review of research on Facebook use. *The Open Communication Journal, 6*(1). https://doi.org/10.2174/1874916X01206010037

Carpenter, J. P., & Krutka, D. G. (2015). Engagement through microblogging: Educator professional development via Twitter. *Professional Development in Education, 41*(4), 707-728. https://doi.org/10.1080/19415257.2014.939294

Chai, J., & Fan, K. (2017). Constructing creativity: Social media and creative expression in design education. *Eurasia Journal of Mathematics, Science and Technology Education, 14*(1), 33-43. https://doi.org/10.12973/ejmste/79321

Cru, J. (2015). Language revitalisation from the ground up: Promoting Yucatec Maya on Facebook. *Journal of Multilingual and Multicultural Development, 36*(3), 284-296. https://doi.org/10.1080/01434632.2014.921184

Cunliffe, D. (2019). Minority languages and social media. In G. Hogan-Brun & B. O'Rourke (Eds.), *The Palgrave handbook of minority languages and communities* (pp. 451-480). Springer. https://doi.org/10.1057/978-1-137-54066-9_18

Dayter, D. (2015). Small stories and extended narratives on Twitter. *Discourse, Context & Media, 10*, 19-26. https://doi.org/10.1016/j.dcm.2015.05.003

DePew, K. E. (2011). Social media at academia's periphery: Studying multilingual developmental writers' Facebook composing strategies. *Reading Matrix: An International Online Journal, 11*(1), 54-75. https://digitalcommons.odu.edu/english_fac_pubs/29

Deschene, D. N. (2019). Coptic language learning and social media. *Languages, 4*(3), 73. https://doi.org/10.3390/languages4030073

Ditchfield, H. (2020). Behind the screen of Facebook: Identity construction in the rehearsal stage of online interaction. *New Media & Society, 22*(6), 927-943. https://doi.org/10.1177/1461444819873644

Ferré-Pavia, C., Zabaleta, I., Gutierrez, A., Fernandez-Astobiza, I., & Xamardo, N. (2018). Internet and social media in European minority languages: Analysis of the digitalization process. *International Journal of Communication, 12*, 1065–1086. https://ijoc.org/index.php/ijoc/article/view/7464/2285

Flew, T. (2018). Social media and the cultural and creative industries. In J. Burgess, A. Marwick, & T. Poell (Eds.), *The SAGE handbook of social media*. Sage.

Giri, P. C., & Rana, K. (2022). Lessons learned from teaching English through Facebook Live for future. *International Journal of Technology in Education and Science (IJTES), 6*(1), 14-31. https://doi.org/10.46328/ijtes.309

Gonzalez-Polledo, E., & Tarr, J. (2016). The thing about pain: The remaking of illness narratives in chronic pain expressions on social media. *New Media & Society, 18*(8), 1455-1472. https://doi.org/10.1177/1461444814560126

Gündüz, U. (2017). The effect of social media on identity construction. *Mediterranean Journal of Social Sciences, 8*(5), 85-85. https://doi.org/10.36941/mjss

Guta, H., & Karolak, M. (2015). Veiling and blogging: Social media as sites of identity negotiation and expression among Saudi women. *Journal of International Women's Studies, 16*(2), 115-127. http://vc.bridgew.edu/jiws/vol16/iss2/7

Hanusch, F., & Tandoc, E. C. (2019). Comments, analytics, and social media: The impact of audience feedback on journalists' market orientation. *Journalism, 20*(6), 695-713. https://doi.org/10.1177/1464884917720305

Honeycutt, C., & Cunliffe, D. (2010). The use of the Welsh language on Facebook: An initial investigation. *Information, Communication & Society, 13*(2), 226-248. https://doi.org/10.1080/13691180902914628

Hutchinson, A. (2020). Facebook closes in on new milestone of 3 billion total users across its platforms. *Social Media Today*. https://about.fb.com/company-info/

Igboanusi, H., & Peter, L. (2004). Oppressing the oppressed: The threats of Hausa and English to Nigeria's minority languages. *International Journal of the Sociology of Language, 2004*(170), 131-140. https://doi.org/10.1515/ijsl.2004.2004.170.131

Jeon, L., & Mauney, S. (2014). *"As much as I love you, I'll never get you to understand": Political discourse and 'face' work on Facebook.* Proceedings of the 22nd Annual Symposium about Language and Society-Austin, Rice University, USA.

Jongbloed-Faber, L., Van de Velde, H., Van der Meer, C., & Klinkenberg, E. (2016). Language use of Frisian bilingual teenagers on social media. *Treballs de sociolingüística catalana*, 27-54. https://raco.cat/index.php/TSC/article/view/316429

Jongbloed-Faber, L., van Loo, J., & Cornips, L. (2017). Regional languages on Twitter: A comparative study between Frisian and Limburgish. *Dutch Journal of Applied Linguistics, 6*(2), 174-196. https://doi.org/10.1177/117718011501100105

Kavakci, E., & Kraeplin, C. R. (2016). Religious beings in fashionable bodies: The online identity construction of hijabi social media personalities. *Media, Culture & Society, 39*(6), 850-868. https://doi.org/10.1177/0163443716679031

Keegan, T. T., Mato, P., & Ruru, S. (2015). Using Twitter in an Indigenous language: An analysis of Te Reo Māori tweets. *AlterNative: An International Journal of Indigenous Peoples, 11*(1), 59-75. https://doi.org/10.1177/117718011501100105

Khabarhub (2022). Six new languages added to the list of languages spoken in Nepal: Number of languages spoken in Nepal reaches 129. https://english.khabarhub.com/2019/05/53137/

Kosinski, M., Matz, S. C., Gosling, S. D., Popov, V., & Stillwell, D. (2015). Facebook as a research tool for the social sciences: Opportunities, challenges, ethical considerations, and practical guidelines. *American Psychologist, 70*(6), 543. https://doi.org/10.1037/a0039210

Kuss, D. J., & Griffiths, M. D. (2017). Social networking sites and addiction: Ten lessons learned. *International Journal of Environmental Research and Public Health, 14*(3), 311. https://doi.org/10.3390/ijerph14030311

Lee, M. (2018). Navigating the social media space for Māori and Indigenous communities. In I. Piven, R. Gandell, M. Lee, & A. M. Simpson (Eds.), *Global perspectives on social media in tertiary learning and teaching: Emerging research and opportunities* (pp. 51-71). IGI Global. https://doi.org/10.4018/978-1-5225-5826-2.ch003

Li, Q., Guo, X., Bai, X., & Xu, W. (2018). Investigating microblogging addiction tendency through the lens of uses and gratifications theory. *Internet Research*. https://doi.org/10.1108/IntR-03-2017-0092

Li, X., & Duan, B. (2018). Organizational microblogging for event marketing: A new approach to creative placemaking. *International Journal of Urban Sciences, 22*(1), 59-79. https://doi.org/10.1080/12265934.2017.134315

Lindgren, S., & Cocq, C. (2017). Turning the inside out: Social media and the broadcasting of Indigenous discourse. *European Journal of Communication, 32*(2), 131-150. https://doi.org/10.1177/0267323116674112

Liu, Z., Min, Q., Zhai, Q., & Smyth, R. (2016). Self-disclosure in Chinese microblogging: A social exchange theory perspective. *Information & Management, 53*(1), 53-63. https://doi.org/10.1016/j.im.2015.08.006

Marchukov, A. (2016). Promoting culture abroad: The experience of Germany and Japan in the field of cultural diplomacy. *Journal of Philological, Educational and Cultural Studies, 1*(2). https://cyberleninka.ru/article/n/promoting-culture-abroad-the-experience-of-germany-and-japan-in-the-field-of-cultural-diplomacy

McDaniel, B. T., Coyne, S. M., & Holmes, E. K. (2012). New mothers and media use: Associations between blogging, social networking, and maternal well-being. *Maternal and Child Health Journal, 16*(7), 1509-1517. https://doi.org/10.1007/s10995-011-0918-2

McMonagle, S., Cunliffe, D., Jongbloed-Faber, L., & Jarvis, P. (2019). What can hashtags tell us about minority languages on Twitter? A comparison of cymraeg, frysk, and gaeilge. *Journal of Multilingual and Multicultural Development, 40*(1), 32-49. https://doi.org/10.1080/01434632.2018.1465429

Meikle, G. (2016). *Social media: Communication, sharing and visibility*. Routledge.

Miller, G. (2016). Social media and creative motivation. In R. Garner (Ed.), *Digital Art Therapy: Material, Methods, and Applications* (pp. 40-53). Jessica Kingsley Publishers.

Outakoski, H., Cocq, C., & Steggo, P. (2018). Strengthening Indigenous languages in the digital age: Social media–supported learning in Sápmi. *Media International Australia, 169*(1), 21-31. https://doi.org/10.1177/1329878X18803700

Page, R. (2010). Re-examining narrativity: Small stories in status updates. *Text & Talk, 30*(4), 423-444. https://doi.org/10.1515/text.2010.021

Phyak, P. (2013). Language ideologies and local languages as the medium-of-instruction policy: A critical ethnography of a multilingual school in Nepal. *Current Issues in Language Planning, 14*(1), 127-143. https://doi.org/10.1080/14664208.2013.775557

Phyak, P. (2015). (En)countering language ideologies: Language policing in the ideospace of Facebook. *Language Policy, 14*(4), 377-395. https://doi.org/10.1007/s10993-014-9350-y

Phyak, P. (2019). Transformation from the bottom up: Ideological analysis with Indigenous youth and language policy justice in Nepal. In T. L. McCarty, S. E. Nicholas, & G. Wigglesworth (Eds.), *A world of Indigenous languages: Politics, pedagogies and prospects for language reclamation* (pp. 194-213). Multilingual Matters. https://doi.org/10.21832/9781788923071-013

Pischlöger, C. (2016). Udmurt on social network sites: A comparison with the Welsh case. In R. Toivanen & J. Saarikivi (Eds.), *Linguistic Genocide or Superdiversity* (pp. 108-132). https://doi.org/10.21832/9781783096060-006

Rahmah, R. E. (2018*). Quickgram for facilitating the students' creative writing tasks*. 2nd English Language and Literature International Conference (ELLiC) Proceedings, Indonesia. https://jurnal.unimus.ac.id/index.php/ELLIC/article/view/3533/3348

Rana, K. (2018). Retention of English language tension in multilingual communities of Nepal: A review of teachers' narratives. *Journal of NELTA, 23*(1-2), 40-53. https://10.3126/nelta.v23i1-2.23347

Rana, K. (2022). How teachers developed remote learning during the Covid-19 crisis: What can we learn from rural teachers in Nepal? In M. Hammond (Ed.), *Supporting remote teaching and learning in developing countries: From the global to the local* (pp. 48-61). British Council. https://www.britishcouncil.org.np/sites/default/files/teaching_learning_book.pdf?fbclid=IwAR3QxkAFWmZT7hxYi4ES2gzQMPinajhyh1un2mcQy50vRzmFjRTQlbx5rVk

Rana, K., & Sah, P. K. (forthcoming). English as a medium of instruction policy in Nepal's higher education. In P. K. Sah & G. Fang (Eds.), *English Medium Instruction in Asian Universities: Policies, Politics, and Ideologies*. Routledge.

Rasheed, M. I., Malik, M. J., Pitafi, A. H., Iqbal, J., Anser, M. K., & Abbas, M. (2020). Usage of social media, student engagement, and creativity: The role of knowledge sharing behavior and cyberbullying. *Computers & Education, 159*, 104002. https://doi.org/10.1016/j.compedu.2020.104002

Ratten, V. (2017). Social media innovations and creativity. In A. Brem & E. Viardot (Eds.), *Revolution of innovation management* (pp. 199-220). Springer. https://doi.org/10.1057/978-1-137-57475-6_8

Rice, E. S., Haynes, E., Royce, P., & Thompson, S. C. (2016). Social media and digital technology use among Indigenous young people in Australia: A literature review. *International Journal for Equity in Health, 15*(1), 81. https://doi.org/10.1186/s12939-016-0366-0

Sah, P. K. (2020). English medium instruction in South Asian's multilingual schools: unpacking the dynamics of ideological orientations, policy/practices, and democratic questions. *International Journal of Bilingual Education and Bilingualism*, 1-14. https://doi.org/10.1080/13670050.2020.1718591

Sauter, T. (2014). What's on your mind? Writing on Facebook as a tool for self-formation. *New Media & Society, 16*(5), 823-839. https://doi.org/10.1177%2F1461444813495160

Shafie, L. A., & Nayan, S. (2013). Languages, code-switching practice and primary functions of Facebook among university students. *Study in English Language Teaching, 1*(1), 187-199.

Sharma, B. K. (2012). Beyond social networking: Performing global Englishes in Facebook by college youth in Nepal 1. *Journal of Sociolinguistics, 16*(4), 483-509. https://doi.org/10.1111/j.1467-9841.2012.00544.x

Sharma, B. K., & Phyak, P. (2017). Neoliberalism, linguistic commodification, and ethnolinguistic identity in multilingual Nepal. *Language in Society, 46*(2), 231-256. https://doi.org/10.1017/S0047404517000045

Shlezak, A. (2015). The narrative discourse in Facebook electronic communication. *Procedia-Social and Behavioral Sciences, 209*, 476-483. https://doi.org/10.1016/j.sbspro.2015.11.259

Stern, A. J. (2017). How Facebook can revitalise local languages: Lessons from Bali. *Journal of Multilingual and Multicultural Development, 38*(9), 788-796. https://doi.org/10.1080/01434632.2016.1267737

Velázquez, I. (2017). Reported literacy, media consumption and social media use as measures of relevance of Spanish as a heritage language. *International Journal of Bilingualism, 21*(1), 21-33. https://doi.org/10.1177/1367006915596377

Waitoa, J., Scheyvens, R., & Warren, T. R. (2015). E-whanaungatanga: The role of social media in Māori political empowerment. *AlterNative: An International Journal of Indigenous Peoples, 11*(1), 45-58. https://doi.org/10.1177/117718011501100104

Wiggers, H. (2017). Digital divide: Low German and other minority languages. *Advances in Language and Literary Studies, 8*(2), 130-142. https://doi.org/10.7575/aiac.alls.v.8n.2p.130

Wu, Y., Li, E. Y., & Chang, W. (2016). Nurturing user creative performance in social media networks. *Internet Research, 26*(4), 869-900. https://doi.org/10.1108/IntR-10-2014-0239

Wyburn, J. (2018). Media pressures on Welsh language preservation. *The Journal of Mathematical Sociology, 42*(1), 37-46. https://doi.org/10.1080/0022250X.2017.1396984

Zhang, Y., & Ren, W. (2020). 'This is so skrrrrr'–creative translanguaging by Chinese micro-blogging users. *International Journal of Multilingualism*, 1-16. https://doi.org/10.1080/14790718.2020.1753746

DIG DHOJ LAWATI is an MPhil scholar in the Faculty of Social Sciences and Education, Nepal Open University, Nepal. His major research interests lie in the area of minority language use in social media, decolonization, post-colonialism, and Indigenous studies. Email: hilihanglawati@gmail.com.

KARNA RANA, PhD, is an Assistant Professor in the Faculty of Social Sciences and Education, Nepal Open University, Nepal. His areas of research interest are online learning, digital technology and education, ICT and education policy, e-based learning, social media in education, language teaching and policy, Indigenous studies, multilingualism and mother-tongue-based education. Email: karnabdr@gmail.com.

Manuscript submitted: **August 17, 2021**
Manuscript revised: **November 4, 2021**
Accepted for publication: **February 4, 2022**

Book Review

© *Journal of Underrepresented and Minority Progress*
Volume 6, Issue 1 (2022), pp. 121-124
ISSN: 2574-3465 Print/ ISSN: 2574-3481 Online
http://ojed.org/jump

Recent Perspectives on Task-Based Language Learning and Teaching

Ahmadian, M. J., & García Mayo, M. D. P. (Eds) (2018). De Gruyter Mouton. ISBN: 978-1501511479

Reviewed By: Krishna Kumari Upadhayaya, Kathmandu University, Nepal

The book, *Recent Perspectives on Task-Based Language Learning and Teaching*, edited by Mohammad Javad Ahmadian and María del Pilar García Mayo, may prove a useful tool for experienced and novice Task-Based Language Teaching (TBLT) researchers. The book is divided into 12 chapters and discusses the most recent trends in TBLT.

First, the foreword section, written by Ali Shehadeh, is a discussion about the importance of TBLT. This section mentions the relevance of TBLT in the field of second language acquisition (SLA). It covers three main themes: TBLT in foreign contexts, TBLT and second language (L 2) writing, and TBLT and technology. He advocates that, TBLT is shifting from second language contexts to foreign language contexts.

The introduction section of the book is written by Ahmadian and García Mayo. They postulate that their inspiration to write the book was to assimilate the epistemological multiplicity of TBLT and SLA by combining different theoretical perspectives. As a result, the book is divided into four major sections covering these four perceptions and their relevant theoretical and empirical foundations.

All four sections have three chapters each. Section 1 is dedicated to the cognitive-interactionist theory as a theoretical framework for TBLT research which demands interaction through pair and small groups. However, the authors point to the gaps that exist in this perspective. TBLT studies related to sociocultural theory and complexity theory are covered respectively in Sections 2 and 3. As claimed by the authors, these two perspectives have opened up new avenues of research in the field of SLA; however, studies from such perspectives are few in TBLT. Section 4 reflects on the pedagogical perspectives to TBLT research. In this section the reader learns that due to the context-sensitivity of both TBLT in general and tasks in particular, studies in different parts of the world may harvest different results.

Section 1, Chapter 1, contains a recent empirical study by prominent scholars, García Mayo, Agirre, and Azkarai. The study is on cognitive-interactionist theory, which investigates two types of task repetition; same task repetition and procedural repetition, influence complexity, accuracy, and fluency in reference to oral production which was tested with young Spanish EFL learners. The findings reveal, procedural task repetition positively impacted the participants' fluency and accuracy. Additionally, it is indicated that task completion in itself can contribute to measures of fluency and accuracy.

Chapter 2 is written by Wen. Here, the author integrates research on formulaic sequences in SLA and cognitive aptitude factors of Working Memory (WM) into L2 task planning and performance. The results of his study, shows the importance of fixed phrases (formulaic sequences) in task performance, he proposes that formulaic sequences have the potential to be integrated into the traditional variables of complexity, accuracy, fluency, and lexis as measures of task performance. Moreover, Wen argues that apart from learning vocabulary and grammar, it would be beneficial for the learners to be taught phrasal knowledge too.

Chapter 3 contains a study by Gurzynski-Weiss, Henderson, and Jung which explores the timing and type of learner modified output in relation to correct perception of feedback in face-to-face and synchronous task-based chat. The findings revealed, learners' immediate output modification strongly correlates with their correct noticing of feedback. In other words, when learners are required to produce immediate partial modified output, they would be more likely to notice feedback, as compared to when they are not required to produce modified output. Interestingly, the relationship between immediate production of modified output and noticing of feedback was more robust in chat rather than face-to-face interactions.

Section 2 (chapters 4 through 6) is designated to sociocultural theory. In chapter 4, Ahmadian and Garcia Mayo contend that tasks require learners to resort to their cognitive and linguistic resources for the sake of mediation, appropriation, and internalization—a belief that elucidates the link between sociocultural theory and TBLT. Chapter 5 outlines the effects of L3 learner proficiency and task types on language mediation. Williams investigates the adoption of Content Based Instruction (CBI) into a TBLT framework in the context of a French curriculum. According to him, CBI can inform and augment TBLT by offering opportunities for the stages in tasks which lack language focus or focus on linguistic elements, particularly in difficult grammatical points or sociolinguistic/pragmatic aspects of language; this focus on language elements, while performing a task, can be directed by a feature typical of CBI (e.g., verbalization).

Chapters 7, 8, 9 fall under section 3. Here the authors draw on the complexity theory framework. By defining tasks as fertile grounds for the integration of social, cognitive, and professional aspects of second/foreign language learning, Bygate (chapter 7) argues, tasks are excellent contexts for the development of learner autonomy. Larsen-freeman and Nguyen (chapter 8), bring into light L2 learners' inter-individual and intra-individual variations of performance on the acquisition of 30 English formulaic sequences by using tasks in the context of the classroom. While Wen's study in Chapter 2 show the significance of formulaic sequences in task performance, the pretest, posttest, and delayed posttest of this study done by Larsen-freeman and Nguyen demonstrated that TBLT is not only useful for teaching grammatical and lexical features, but also for teaching formulaic sequences. By looking at TBLT from an ecological viewpoint in Chapter 9, Kramsch and Narcy-Combes suggest, empathy has to be incorporated into TBLT.

Section 4 (chapter 10) delves into TBLT from a pedagogical and educational perspective. For example, East pinpoints the relationship between tasks and explicit grammar teaching by comparing the strong form of TBLT, which is a 'zero grammar' approach, with weaker versions of

TBLT, describing focus on form, and focus on meaning. Due to teachers' lack of understanding with tasks, Müller-Hartmann and Schocker (chapter 11) argue that long-term teacher training programs that promote teachers' reflective ability are more facilitative than one-shot in-service training sessions that focus on theoretical input. Finally, Newton and Bui (chapter 12) conducted a Vietnamese study in which the researchers evaluated the principles of a newly developed curriculum against the established principles of TBLT.

This book can be of great use for the teachers who are interested applying TBLT in their teaching practice. Yet, we can't deny the fact that we are living in the era of science and technology and the teaching modes have been changing from face-to-face to distance and online teaching which was not covered in this text.

Krishna Kumari Upadhayaya is a PhD student in English Language Education at Kathmandu University. She has published four school level books and has been providing training to English language teachers since 2009. During the Covid-19 pandemic, she conducted research on effective teaching methods for online modalities. She has given two international presentations on the same topic for Kent University, UK and TEFL Kuwait so far. Her recent achievement is a training from OPEN Winter 2022 Course on Creating and Implementing Online Courses. Her email address is krisna_phele21@kusoed.edu.np.

Manuscript submitted: ***December 31, 2021***
Manuscript revised: ***February 4, 2022***
Accepted for publication: ***March 5, 2022***

www.ingramcontent.com/pod-product-compliance
Lightning Source LLC
Chambersburg PA
CBHW060806050426
42449CB00008B/1556